DYING TO BE

enough

Kristin DiDomenico

Michele,
Thank you
for being on
this journey of
"Becoming Enough"
Love
Kristin D.

Printed in the United States of America

www.kristinfitness.com

ISBN: 978-0-578-42460-6

for my family

You were there, all along

acknowledgements

Thank you to my husband Pat and my children,
Megan and Kevin, for their support through this journey
and reminding me why I am writing this book.

Thank you to my friends Karen and Rochelle
for their talent, guidance, and encouraging me
to share my why.

Thank you to Bonnie, my book coach, for editing and providing
the framework in which I could express my vision.

Thank you to my close friends and clients who have
given me the strength and reassurance to live my why.

And always, thank you to God for the subtle, and not so subtle,
messages that keep me on the *real* path.

Note: Some names in the book have been changed.

preface

This book is about my physical death during a trail race in 2014, my 2% chance of miracle survival ... and the in between. It's about how my physical death on that gravel trail in Reston, Virginia, forced me to examine the "little deaths" in my life—the abrupt ending of my Olympic figure skating dream at age 15 and the addictions, self-abuse and challenges that ultimately led me to that fateful day and then the reawakening of self.

This book is also about where I visited when my body lay lifeless on that trail. During my near-death experience, I felt the peace that awaits us on the other side of this world. I was given a sneak peak of sorts. Hope. A second chance. Today, my husband calls me Kristin 2.0.

I believe we are all here for a purpose. I share here with you my sometimes-ugly insides that I wanted (and still want) to hide from the world and from me. As I shared my story with others, it seemed to offer a connection to their own struggles in life and the hope that they were not alone. My experiences are no greater or lesser than yours. I don't share my story for pity. There are many who have suffered far worse. I believe that my ups and downs were all a part of a bigger plan—the plan that I did not write.

I wrote this to offer hope to those who suffer inside quietly, and push through life to get through it and struggle in the present. Pain and struggle are part of the human experience. None of us are immune from it. I share what happened in my life leading up to the day of my sudden cardiac death and then how that experience has helped me to live life on life's terms by shedding those outer layers that have held me back from joy. You may not relate to my experiences, but you may relate on some level to how I felt. I do feel vulnerable to share me, but I also believe that if one person can gain hope—or a willingness to share their story with another person—then I have done my job.

TRAIL RU

696:
MY RACE NUMBER FROM THAT
FATEFUL DAY. AN OMEN?

one

DR. TEVAR: MY GUARDIAN ANGEL

1

THE DAY
EVERYTHING CHANGED

I've competed in hundreds of races, including two Ironman triathlons and the Duathlon World Championships. I am a health coach and personal trainer. Fitness is my career and my passion. On paper I have done everything I was supposed to do to be physically healthy. So it's ironic that my ultimate undoing would be a local, casual trail race with a bunch of girlfriends.

On Sunday, Oct. 19, 2014, I died. In that moment I was forced to let go completely from this world and everything that I have in it. After years of fighting for control, I realized I had none. I had no choice. I had to give up. My strength ultimately led to my realization that I am powerless. I surrendered. In that moment I was given a sneak peak of sorts. Hope.

That morning before I left for the race, my husband, Pat, and I were talking about the fact that this was the first trail race in a while that he wouldn't be running with me. We enjoy a little healthy competition and have fun running together. But this would be a girls' outing with the group of women that I had trained and travelled with for the Ironman. We dubbed ourselves the "Iron Maidens."

Trail running offers a different kind of challenge from road racing, as you must navigate hidden roots, rocks, and uneven terrain. A year ago at the same race, I had fallen and twisted my ankle. Pat had helped me back to my feet and walked with me until I was able to start running again. On this morning, a year later, I said to him, "What if something happens to me ... you won't be there this time." We chuckled.

Laurie, Kirsten, Lori, and Jill picked me up about an hour before the race, and together we drove to pick up our friend Annie. It was a beautiful fall morning. Physically, I was feeling nothing out of the ordinary. I was ready to run and have a good time with friends.

The six of us giggled and were delighted at how we all managed to get together for the race. We were looking forward to a hearty breakfast after the race. The group playfully teased me about the various hydrating drinks and potions I had packed to make me run fast!

Arriving to pick up our bib numbers at the check-in table, I was handed #696, which I thought was just a bit too close to 666, the number of the devil. At check-in, I immediately asked at the check-in table if I could have a different number. I was told they couldn't change anything at that point.

As we were warming up and pinning our numbers to our clothes, I told my friends that I hoped my race number wasn't an omen. Jill offered to switch numbers with me. We joked and I said it would be fine.

Looking back, I wonder if the number *was* some kind of warning, or just an odd coincidence. Another odd thing: I had forgotten my heart-rate monitor that morning, something I otherwise wear without fail. I chalked my mistake up to being immersed in the moment with friends and decided to just enjoy the race free from technology.

The six of us walked to the starting line where a few hundred other runners were gathered. Since we were not running for time or to be competitive, there was no warm-up. We just began running.

The race started off with a giant hill. On this particular day, I was in a mode of going with the flow—not my normal "race" mode. I caught up with another friend and client, Kim, who had participated in one of my running groups. Kim urged me to go ahead and run my pace rather than stay with her. She was doing the 5-mile race, while I was doing a second loop with the 10-mile runners.

After that first lap, I actually contemplated finishing the 5-mile distance with Kim. Once we were approaching the 5-mile finish, however, I decided to continue on. It was a beautiful day, and I would enjoy spending a few more miles in nature. Typical for me, I needed to keep moving just a little bit longer.

If I was feeling "off" that day, I don't remember. The way I recall it, one minute I was running, and the next I wasn't. At about the 9½-mile mark, I veered off the trail to the left, feeling light-headed and dizzy. And then I dropped. I must have gone down slowly, steadying myself with my hands, as I had no major scratches or bumps from a hard fall. I felt no pain. I felt nothing. Just "lights out."

Chaos erupted on the trail. Other runners were screaming for help, unsure of what had happened. There was a sense of disorganized directives, shock, and uncertainty of what to do next. As I lay in semi-consciousness, unable to get any words out to tell them what to do, I became aware on some level that I could do nothing. I had to let go. That was my last earthly memory.

Within minutes, my guardian angel came upon the scene. Dr. Rahul Tevar is a surgeon who lives in Washington, D.C., and works in suburban Maryland. He had never run a trail race before that day.

What brought Dr. Tevar so far beyond the Beltway to this race on this day, and why was such a skilled person running behind me at the precise moment I most needed him? What if I hadn't slowed down to run with my friend, Kim? What if I had finished at the 5-mile mark? Multiple small decision points put the doctor and me together at the right time.

These decision points were not accidents or coincidences. I believe God had His hand in the order of events that day. Dr. Tevar was put there to save my life. I can't count the number of solo training runs I have taken deep into the woods, or the lake swims that I have done with a few friends. It is a miracle that my life-threatening heart rhythm malfunction occurred when and where it did.

To put this in perspective, consider the 2% survival rate of individuals who have sudden cardiac death outside the walls of a hospital (that's what happened to me). We calculated that it was about two or three minutes before Dr. Tevar ran upon the chaotic scene. He heard people shouting and looking for someone with a cell phone to call for help. He described my breathing pattern as "agonal breathing, the final breaths before someone dies." And then I stopped breathing. The doctor could not find a pulse. He immediately began CPR to keep my blood circulating and getting to my brain. Without the flow of oxygen, brain damage occurs within a couple of minutes.

Dr. Tevar handed someone his phone to call 911. Meanwhile, the race director, Jim Harmen, had received word of what had happened. As I lay lifeless on the ground, Jim ran to his car to get a portable defibrillator and rushed back to the scene to deliver it. Luckily, I was only a ¼ mile from the finish line when I collapsed.

I was told it took about 10 minutes before the defibrillator arrived. Another runner, who had recently taken a CPR class, applied the electrode stickers as Dr. Tevar continued CPR. He pressed the button that sent a life-saving 700-volt shock to my heart. But I wasn't out of the woods yet. Dr. Tevar said, "It is a matter of minutes between life and death without CPR and use of the defibrillator."

The paramedics arrived soon after, and I was loaded into an ambulance and whisked away to Reston Hospital. My skin was as grey as the sky before a thunderstorm, but my heart was now beating, albeit erratically. I was still unconscious and, being without a natural heartbeat for about 10 minutes, the paramedics wondered aloud how much brain damage had occurred. Dr. Tevar later said that he thought my survival rate as they loaded me into the ambulance was "somewhere near 50-50."

Looking back, I had experienced a couple of warning signs. The day before the race, I had seen a strange flash of light as I was coaching my running group. The flash was brief and startling. I didn't think much of it. A night about a year before that, I had gotten up in the middle of the night to go to the bathroom and passed out on the bathroom floor. I went back to bed, thinking it was nothing to worry about. The next day I did a 100-mile bike ride without a thought that I could be in danger. These two episodes, doctors have told me, were most likely the same heart rhythm malfunction. But it was not time yet.

My doctors told me the fateful episode was likely triggered by the consecutive days of hot yoga classes I took the week before the race. The owner of a studio had offered me a spot in their "30-day challenge" (30 classes in 30 days). Before that, I took one or two hot yoga classes a week, never a class every day.

In hot yoga, you go through a series of postures that challenge the body through strength and flexibility—in a room heated to 106 degrees. I saw this as a supplement to my triathlon training. I loved to sweat and challenge my body to improve and withstand discomfort. More was never enough.

The topic of heart disease and its potential ravages was a familiar topic in my home. My father had died eight years earlier from a heart attack, in part because of unhealthy habits, and I was determined to live differently. Exercise was supposed to protect my heart, not hurt it!

I knew I had a heart defect, but specialists had cleared me for vigorous exercise. I had no idea that the structure of my heart couldn't handle rapid fluid loss. After hot yoga classes, I typically felt very sluggish and struggled to rehydrate, even with a constant intake of fluid replacement. I didn't know this wasn't normal.

Meanwhile, while my life was slipping away on a dirt trail in the Reston woods, my family was enjoying a relaxing Sunday morning at home—blissfully unaware of the phone call that was about to come.

The race director, having found my emergency contact on the reverse side of my 696 bib number, dialed the phone and relayed just the facts to Pat, wanting to stress the severity of the situation. "Your wife has collapsed in the race. Her heart is not beating. They have the defibrillator and are trying to get her heart started again. An ambulance is here and you need to get to Reston Hospital now."

Pat grabbed the kids and one other thing on the way out the door—the "heart file." It included the result of tests on my heart from a decade earlier, when I had been diagnosed with hypertrophic cardiomyopathy (HCM)—a thickening of the left ventricle.

After a past incident of arrhythmia—nowhere near the severity of this episode—I had gone through a series of tests. The specialists concluded that the incident had been due to a genetic HCM, not a weak or damaged heart. In fact, doctors said I had a very strong heart and gave me the green light not only to exercise, but to continue training at a high intensity and continue to compete.

A doctor at John's Hopkins had examined every angle of my heart in 2007. I recall seeing the image of my pumping heart up on a giant television screen. The doctor pointed to the thickness and assured us that there was no risk of sudden death because of the location of that thickness—in the apex (or tip) of the heart. He said I would be more likely to die by "stepping off the curb and getting hit by a bus."

When that figurative bus hit on October 19, my husband thought of that doctor visit as he grabbed the heart file and ran out the door. "This can't be happening—those doctors said she would be fine," he thought.

The drive from our home in Potomac Falls to Reston is about 20 minutes. But those 20 minutes felt like 20 years for my family, not knowing what they would find when they got to the hospital. Describing the moment, Pat told me later,

> *We all held hands and prayed. It was like having everything you know about your life pulled out*

*from under you. You see your whole plan of
life—growing old with someone, sharing in your
children's adult experiences ... travel ... grand-
children. It felt like I was drowning ... like normal
life was above me and I wanted to get back to
it. It was as if I was watching a movie. It seemed
unreal. Then came the feelings of regret: Did I
tell her I loved her this morning? Did she know
how much I loved her? Why didn't we do X, Y,
or Z when we had the time? Did I let her know
how important she was to me? What was our last
conversation?*

As he drove, Pat felt things slipping away. "My mind went to
raising our kids without their mom." His long life vision felt under
attack. This was not supposed to happen.

My children, Megan and Kevin (18 and 15 at the time) were
experiencing similar feelings. Megan was in the room with my
husband when he got "the call." She knew from his tone that
something wasn't right. As Megan told me later,

*I was crying. I was confused because you are so
healthy. Then I got angry—why did this have
to happen? I started to imagine you not being
there and then got really sad. Things that seemed
important a few minutes before didn't seem so
important anymore.*

Kevin was in the shower when the call came. My husband's
loud knock and tone startled him. Kevin's first thought was that I

had gotten hurt falling down in the race. I had crashed in a bike race a few years earlier, and Kevin thought we were in for another afternoon of stitches. But as he told me later,

> *In the car I realized it was much more serious.*
> *The car ride was really scary, but I mostly felt*
> *blank and didn't want to think about it.*

When the three of them walked into the hospital, I was flat out on bed—no movement. Doctors, nurses, and paramedics were swarming around me, busy at work.

My first conscious memory after the collapse was Megan grabbing my ice-cold hand. I turned my head and asked, "Is that my family?"

serenity prayer

God, grant me The serenity to accept the things I cannot change; The courage to change the things I can; The wisdom to know the difference. Living one day at a time; Enjoying one moment at a time; Accepting hardship as the pathway to peace; Taking, as He did, this sinful world as it is, not as I would have it; Trusting that He will make all things right if I surrender to His will; That I may be reasonably happy in this life, and supremely happy with Him forever in the next.

—Reinhold Niehbur

LITTLE KRISTIN AGE 3 ON
SINGLE-BLADE SKATES:
I LOVED SKATING FROM
THE MOMENT I STEPPED ON
THE ICE.

two

AGE 10:
PHOTO FOR THE
LOCAL NEWSPAPER

MY FIRST LOVE
SET THE PATTERN

During my childhood in northern New Jersey, there was an outdoor skating pond down the street. As soon as the pond froze over, I begged to get on the ice. I remember the excitement I felt deep in my belly when the green "safe to skate" flag was run up the flagpole. My mother took my younger sister, Lauren, on the Radio Flyer sled as I, age 5, ventured off on my single-blade skates. I loved skating and couldn't get enough.

At age 7, I joined my first group skating lesson. I remember showing up to find everyone else in fancy skating dresses and knowing how to do a two-foot spin. I arrived in my Toughskins jeans, and the only thing spinning was my head. I was immediately frustrated at how far behind the learning curve I felt. I expected to be able to do what the other girls were doing, no matter what. I was already determined and driven to measure up.

As I began to improve and glide across the ice with more ease, I felt free and alive. It was a freedom and an escape. The music, the chill of the ice rink, and even the smell of the hot pretzels and french fries from the snack bar appealed to my senses. I was home. Not to mention the competition with the other girls. I wanted to be better from my first day. I would work hard day-in-day-out with one goal in mind—to be the best.

Being the best became my obsession—because even as a young child, I felt it was my responsibility to fix my family. My family was in pain, and I was convinced that being the best ice skater possible—an Olympic champion—was the path to deflect the pain and heal my family. The burden was heavy, and the drive intense.

I recall one day that my parents were fighting upstairs in their bedroom. Lauren and I sat on the stairs holding our ears and each other in fear. She was 5 and I was 7 years old. I felt responsible. If I were better behaved, followed directions, and treated my sister better, things would be different. Another time when I was 9 years old, my father and mother were arguing and my father walked out, saying he was leaving us. I ran after him and begged him to stay, not to go away. He ignored me. My mother came outside and told me that this was between the two of them and not to get involved. I felt alone and helpless, out of control. I wanted to make things better, and I was going to do so. If I could just divert attention away from the family problems, everything would be okay.

Throughout my childhood, my father worked, smoked, overate, and drank, all to excess. He was moody and had outbursts of anger that scared and upset me—but he could also be like a teddy bear. I didn't understand why he would come home from work early and take a long nap. Or come home because he didn't feel well. Or, worse yet, show up in a rage, yelling at my mother or one of us.

My father often berated my mother about the house being a mess, dinner being cold, or the meat overcooked. The yelling would end with him storming off without eating. It was scary, but my siblings and I learned to cope by pretending it wasn't happening.

My mother worked to keep my father happy, or at least not hurtful or angry. Most times, she failed and became the target of his rage. My sister and I, and eventually our brother Craig, would watch and beg my father to stop. Eventually, Dad would flee the scene, leaving his verbal debris in a heap on the floor for all of us to pick up. My mom tried hard to keep it together for all of us, and none of us ever talked about the harm that my father was inflicting on her or us.

Looking back, I realize that one of my mother's coping mechanisms was the glass of wine she hid in the corner of the kitchen counter. She would continue to pour that first glass of wine over and over.

As a young child, I didn't know that all the drinking was abnormal. I did know that my family was broken, and I was convinced it was my job to fix it.

I didn't connect easily with my mother. She didn't seem to know me or see the pain that was ever-present in me, but she had keen eyes for any pain that I caused her. As the oldest in the family, I was repeatedly told that I should know better. I wasn't sure what I was supposed to know, which made the accusation hurt even more. I was told that it was my job to set a good example for my sister. I didn't like my sister—because she stole away any atten-tion that was available from my mother. I constantly got in trouble for hurting Lauren and mistreating her when we were young. She would tease and annoy me until I would act out and hurt her physically, leaving her in tears and me in trouble.

I connected more easily with my dad, and he with me. He would give me long-winded pep talks about being the best and always striving to achieve. I soaked up his words, certain that if I were the best, I'd win his love. I'd do anything for that.

My father taught me to believe in myself, but his expectations—or the way I interpreted them—were unrealistic. I was a good skater, but striving to be the best in a pool of millions of other girls set me up for disappointment. Not knowing this, I would spend several years working hard to gain my coveted trophy—my father's love. Ice skating was the venue, but my father's approval was the goal.

I wanted to go to the Olympics and be like Dorothy Hamill, my idol. I had her haircut. I also wanted her cool glasses with big frames. So in the third grade, I purposefully failed the eye exam at school.

The school nurse called my mother, telling her to make an optometrist appointment as soon as possible. The optometrist did a test that quickly revealed my lie. No Dorothy Hamill glasses for me. My mother was horrified and embarrassed. I was punished. Even at a young age, I knew what I wanted and was willing to go to extremes to get it.

Around that time, my father, who had a construction business, built our house in Manasquan, a suburb near the Jersey Shore. His business was taking off and our family had outgrown our home in Madison, New Jersey. I was 9 years old, Lauren was 7, Craig was 3, and my mother was pregnant. I remember she had the flu and was sick for much of this time. The move to the new house was stressful. My dad was working all hours while my mother was trying to manage three small kids and my skating practices, which were increasing in number, length, and cost.

My brother, Ryan, was born in November of 1978, with a serious virus. Ryan survived, but he remained in the intensive care unit for weeks. After a few months, Ryan, who had been diagnosed as developmentally delayed, was failing to thrive. My mother poured everything into his care. The situation was difficult on all of us, but my mother suffered the most.

My parents hired a private coach for me, and I began practicing three times a week. I passed the tests to qualify for my first United States Figure Skating Association (USFSA) competition. I was ready to compete in the New Jersey Council of Figure Skating Clubs competition in the Juvenile Ladies category.

My Aunt Gail, a seamstress, made my skating dresses. She was a strong woman with strong opinions. One day, Aunt Gail casually commented that I looked "chunky" in a dress I wore for Easter Sunday. While this was a throwaway comment for her, it watered an already-present seed of self-loathing about my body. Aunt Gail's words became like a large ball of Velcro to which every negative thought would stick and accumulate.

Concern about how others viewed my weight and how I looked on the ice contributed to a growing lack of self-acceptance and a distorted body image. Still, I tried to stuff those feelings down inside and focus on the task at hand—my first competition.

I felt tremendous anxiety as my name was announced and I stepped onto the ice at the Mennen Arena in Morristown, New Jersey. The rink seemed so big, and I felt so small. I feared disappointing my friends and relatives who had come out to watch me for the first time.

My performance at that first competition was a disaster. I spent more time sliding across the ice than I did on my feet. I finished 13th out of 15 competitors in my category. I was depleted, ashamed, and embarrassed. I had failed. My light had been snuffed out.

At home, Ryan was not making progress as we had hoped. My mom, being fully absorbed in Ryan's care, was oblivious to the pain and pressure I was feeling. Dad, on the other hand, was tuned in to me, at least to my skating. His words after that first skating failure were simple and profound. He told me to come back and "get 'em' next year," to use the experience to help me work harder and return the following year and win. I now had a goal. I worked hard over the next 12 months to please my father and achieve my goal.

The next year, I did return to that same competition. I was again scared and afraid, but I had the experience of the past year under my belt. My dad took me outside shortly before I was to go on the ice for my warm-up. I was in my skates and all ready to go on. But I was beyond nervous. So my dad taught me something he called the "gorilla jump," something I would use before all future competitions.

I jumped up and down like a gorilla for a good 30 seconds. This allowed me to shake off some of my nerves and focus my energy on the task at hand, my performance. And it worked! I made it onto the podium to receive my first bronze medal. It was the first time I learned that hard work and dedication really do pay off.

My laser focus on goals and achievement became a pattern for my years ahead. I had a deep need to prove myself to my father. He was my cheerleader, my voice, my mirror, my strength.

I yearned for his attention and ultimately his love. I had found a way to get it. Temporarily.

With my mother working diligently to help Ryan, my father poured himself into supporting my skating. By age 11, my competing had taken me around the Jersey tristate area and beyond. My alarm would buzz at 5:30 a.m. I'd wake my dad to drive me to the rink for a two-hour practice before school. Some days, I went to practice after school. Some days both. Every Saturday, my dad and I drove two hours away so I could spend the day with the best coaches in the area. Dad wanted to make sure I had an opportunity to succeed. He was an all-or-nothing kind of father. And with skating, we were all in.

During our car rides, Dad lectured me about work ethic and how I needed to do my best to be the best. I would try to express my anxious feelings, and he would respond with cliché expressions like "You are what you do" (not how you feel), "Look through the windshield, not the rear view mirror," and "Plan your work and work your plan." Dad loved a good motto.

Many of our car rides ended with me in tears as I feared I was not good enough in my father's eyes. I needed to try harder. There was not much room for enjoyment and fun, just discipline and competition. But during one car ride my father told me, "You are my favorite child—you are just like me."

During the summer when I was 10 years old, I had my first summer-away skating experience at a camp. I was so young, mixed in with older kids, so I learned a lot besides how to skate better. I learned what homosexuality was, since a few boys allegedly had same-sex preferences. I learned how to juggle, play jacks, and do Chinese jump rope. My dad would visit and take me to his favorite diner, where we would eat club sandwiches and

MY FIRST SKATING DRESS, MADE BY
AUNT GAIL!

rice pudding. This would later become my favorite pre-competition meal. Normal activities mixed in with a lot of skating made this camp fun and increased my love of skating. Back at home that fall, I continued to skate before and after school. I began to enter more local competitions and do well. I was improving, which drove me to work even harder.

The next summer, so that I could be closer to better practice facilities and the best coaches, my parents arranged for me to live on Long Island with a family, the Sampsons. I was 11 years old, on my own, a little girl living away from home.

I recall nights of loneliness and fear. One night I watched *Night of the Living Dead* on television and went to bed, alone, in my room. I cried in fear that zombies would come to my window that night. I stuffed my head under my pillow and tried to push the fear away. That summer, I learned to suppress a lot of sadness and loneliness. I began to ignore my feelings and just "get through" them.

The Sampson family also had a skater, a boy about my age. After a bad practice, his father would yell at him and sometimes beat him. I would go into my room and hide. I was afraid. While I never got hit, I also lacked any sense of comfort from an adult. I only felt the pressure to keep trying harder to be the best.

At daily practices, most of the girls' mothers were there with them. With my mother absent, I felt left out and alone. When my mother came to a competition, my feelings would come out as anger toward her. I would treat her terribly. She would step in and try to mother me. I would not hear of it. I had learned how to take care of myself (or so I thought), and I did not need her. Out of guilt, perhaps, she took it.

Since my father was verbally abusive to my mother, I felt entitled to treat her poorly, too. She was the dumping ground for my inner rage and uncontrollable anger. What was I so angry about? I needed a full-time mother, and it felt like I got a part-time invader. Feeling like my mother didn't know or understand me, I put up a wall at a young age. It would get thicker and thicker as the years went by.

By age 12, I began to understand that competition inside and outside the rink was cutthroat—maybe not to the Tonya Harding-Nancy Kerrigan level, but close. At the 1979 Middle Atlantic Figure Skating Championships, a girl had one of her skates stolen. She had been in first place after the qualifying round and now wasn't able to continue. It was scary and unbelievable that someone would do this. I became aware that some girls (and their parents) would stop at nothing to win—even going so far as crushing the dream of a fellow competitor.

At about this time, my father decided to take my skating to the next level. He put our house on the market and planned to move the family to Colorado or Atlanta, two major hubs for producing the best figure skaters in the country. He also saw both cities as good options to transfer his construction business.

I felt my inner self-importance growing as my skating was taking a front seat in our family. It felt as if I was in charge of the direction we were taking. The weight of that responsibility was crushing for a preteen. Eventually, new developments with Ryan shifted our plans, and the house came off the market. We would need to look at other options. At this point, my father and I were traveling more for practice time and coaching. I spent school vacations and both weekend days in New York with prestigious coaches.

My dresses were now handmade by a seamstress who was well known for making skating dresses. I also wore custom-made skates—one for figures and one set for freestyle. The cost of ice time, training camps, competitions, travel, coaching and equipment—not to mention the time commitment on my family's part—were beginning to mount.

At home it was always tense, especially when my mom and dad were both there. My father practiced what he preached about hard work, but he also brought stress home from work and unloaded it on my mother. He frequently complained about dinner. Dad criticized and belittled Mom for the house being a mess or the kids not being dressed appropriately for dinner. There was a "not good enough" theme being played out daily and we were the actors.

My father yelled at my mother and, in turn, she nagged. But when they weren't going at each other, the kids were in the firing zone. Many times it was a domino effect of sorts—my father would take his frustrations out on my mother, my mother on me, and me on my siblings, especially Lauren.

While my home life was unsettling, I felt in control and successful on the ice. Also, when my parents were focused on my skating, they didn't fight. I felt a sense of power—and pressure—to make everything better for the family.

At age 12, my training was leading up to the big South Atlantic Regional Figure Skating Championships. The top three finishers in the intermediate ladies category—the entry level—would continue on to compete in the Eastern U.S. Figure Skating Championships in Massachusetts. Easterns was a long shot for me because it was my first time at this level of competition.

Back then, the first part of the competition was compulsory figures, where you draw and then trace figure eights with your skate blade. Each level of mastery, from the intermediate to the senior level, would increase the complexity of the circles. We were judged on the parallel line up, inside or outside edges, sizing, and how exact the tracing of the circles were completed. The goal was perfection. While the compulsory figures are no longer included in USFSA competition today, they were my specialty. After the first round of compulsories, I sat in 1st place.

The second portion of the competition was free skate. I completed a three-minute program with a combination of spins, jumps, and footwork to music. I performed well again and held second place after the freestyle portion in the qualifying round, which allowed me to move on to the final round of competition. There were 12 of us in the final round and the top three would move on to Easterns.

I placed second in the final round of compulsories and went on to finish third overall. I still remember standing in the group of girls squeezing through to look for my name on the posted list of finalists. I had made it to Easterns! I was elated! My hard work was paying off, and I was hungry for more.

On the ride home, my father talked with me about the offer one of the top coaches in Atlanta had made. She was interested in coaching me, but I would need to move to Atlanta. The coach offered to set up living arrangements for me with a family and handle my schooling and other logistics. But this required that she take legal guardianship of me. The coach told my father that I had potential to compete at a national and even Olympic level, but I would have to be willing to give up having a normal 12-year-old girl's life.

With the strain that skating was taking on the family, it seemed like the perfect option. I *begged* for the opportunity. Without a second thought, this was what I wanted. This is what I needed. I would train to be the best! This would be the answer to making my family okay and everyone happier. I would be an Olympian!

My mother didn't want me to go, but she did not fight it. She later told me that she closed the blinds on me and tried not to think about it. She didn't want to stand in my way.

After a sixth place finish at Easterns, during the middle of my seventh grade year, I moved in with the Moses family in Atlanta. Their 16-year-old daughter, Lauren, also skated. They lived on a farm with horses, and I had my own suite in the house on the lower level. Mrs. Moses gave me more attention than I was used to receiving. She watched my practices, drove me to school, fed me, and made sure I went to bed on time. I was on a tight schedule. Three different coaches were directing me—one for compulsories, jumps and spins; one for choreography; and one for off-ice training. My life was not mine.

In Atlanta, I skated, went to school, headed back to the rink to skate again, then went home for dinner, homework and bed—only to get up and do it all again. The daily competitive atmosphere was at a much higher level than what I was used to back home. I was no longer the star. My competitors were also my friends, but we all wanted to win. It was pretty cutthroat, as we were all vying for that special attention and praise. I rarely was the recognized one, so I worked harder in hopes to be seen. Practices were long and challenging. I had lost my lead role on center stage. I was just another cast member.

For meals at the Moses' house, I was usually alone in another room while the family ate together. I called home on Wednesday and Sunday evenings. It was all part of the script I followed. As you can guess, Lauren Moses was not a big fan of mine. She also skated, but she did not enjoy it and did not compete. She skated mostly because her mother wanted her to. Once I arrived on the scene, Mrs. Moses had what she had always wanted, a surrogate daughter who loved to skate and had promise. I was her pet project.

At 14 years old, I was on track to go to the U.S. Figure Skating Championships. But, for the first time, my body began to fail me. What started as a nagging pain in my ankle gradually became a case of tendonitis and, eventually, debilitating pain. But the priority was getting me to Nationals no matter what. That meant medication, ice, therapy, and eventually a cortisone shot. I vividly remember being on the doctor's table while the doctor was on the phone with my parents, getting permission to proceed with the shot. After the shot, the pain was still present, but dulled. The competition season would be over in three months; this was my chance, and I had to go for it.

Injuries weren't my only physical troubles. My body shape had begun to shift. I grew hips and breasts, two unwelcome attributes for figure skaters. One day, when I was 13, while in a bathroom stall at the ice rink, I got my period. I did not know what was happening to me or what I was supposed to do. My mother was hundreds of miles away so I confided in another skater, and she helped me figure it out. I didn't understand or like the changes taking place in my body.

At the same time, other things started to shift. I was developing an interest in boys, social life, and fun—three distractions not permitted for competitive figure skaters (at least according to their coaches). These things were not in line with my mission to make it to Nationals. Internally, I began to resent skating. I wanted to be with the other kids, going to football games, the movies, and parties with friends. But I had made my choice, and there was no turning back.

I remember coming home for a break at Christmas. My skating success was bringing me closer to my Olympic dream, but for the first time I felt like I wanted to get out. Skating had become a job with no time off.

I didn't dare mention these feelings to my father. I didn't want to let him down. He had given me what I wanted, what I had begged for. I feared disappointing him and losing his love and attention. He had talked about how skating would be my ticket to life and a world of opportunity. I felt trapped with no way out.

While driving to the airport after Christmas break, I started crying. My father told me I did not need to go back to Atlanta, but he may as well have been speaking a different language. I did not see quitting as an option. I did not want to go back, but I didn't want to stay at home. I was Kristin the skater, like it or not. I would ignore my feelings, bury them inside, and keep going.

In order to keep my focus where it belonged, I was enrolled in private/professional high school. This was a "school" made up of skaters, ballerinas, gymnasts, tennis players—all young kids on the path to athletic stardom. I remember feeling unsure about this switch. My father had always said school comes first, but we knew that wasn't the real truth down here.

This shift was the start of a downward spiral. The more my life focus became narrowed, the more I grew tired of the sport. The better I got at skating, the more I hated it. How could I stop now? My family had spent too much time and money to get me to this point.

The loss of control in my life began to eat at me. I felt like a robot, doing what I was told every minute of every day. Pain or no pain, happy or sad, I needed to perform. I was a machine and machines don't feel.

One day my coach decided to weigh each of her skaters. Some of us needed to lose weight, she said. No names were mentioned, but I knew the coach was talking about me. I did not know where to turn so I turned on myself. I must be punished for allowing this to happen. I had no other answer.

With Mrs. Moses' support, I was put on a diet and began to find a new focus. Maybe I wasn't going to be the best skater, but I was going to be the skinniest. Once I started to see the results of my efforts, I was on a new mission.

I would lock myself in my room after eating as little as I could get away with and do calisthenics for as long as I could to burn the calories I had consumed. I had a list of calories for all foods and would do the math to figure out how long I needed to run in place or how many sit-ups I needed to do to get rid of what I had consumed. This gave me the illusion of control and made me believe, at least temporarily, that I could do anything I set my mind to.

I was now at the level of competition just below the senior category, where I would be eligible for the Olympics. My weight was back down and I was ready, except that the nagging ankle pain had re-emerged.

My mom met me in Philadelphia for the qualifying competition to go to the next level before Nationals. I was extremely nervous and felt a lot of pressure to perform. This was it. This was what I had been working toward and what I had always wanted. But now I wasn't sure. It felt like I had the weight of the world on my shoulders, and I couldn't hold it any more. And my darn ankle was hurting.

I took my anger out on my mom. I felt that she had abandoned me and now she wanted to be my mother. I wanted nothing to do with her, and yet I needed her more than ever. I resented her for trying to walk back into my life and play mom. I was suffering inside, but I didn't know how to lean on her for support or comfort.

During practice sessions, my ankle began to throb in pain. Thinking it must be nerves, I tried not to focus on the pain. I was taped up and icing in hopes that I could make it through the competition and get another cortisone shot to get me through the season. I feared the pain, but focused on mind over matter, as I had been trained.

By the time my father arrived, I was extremely nervous. I needed his approval and felt pressure mounting inside to get it. It felt like my life was on the line. My fear was so big that I remember bursting into tears before leaving for the rink to compete. Even the gorilla jump didn't work. All the ice time, equipment, coaching, housing, and schooling had come down to less than four minutes on the ice. Would I be good enough? Would my dad be proud of me?

In the final round after compulsories, I was in fifth place, not a good sign as this was my strong suit. We had hoped I would take a big lead before heading into the two rounds of freestyle competition. The next day when I began my short program, my left leg gave out in the middle of my routine. My body had given up on me. I had believed in my body's invicibility, and it failed me. As the music played on, I stood motionless and in tears in the middle of the ice. I hobbled off the ice, crying out of embarrassment and defeat. I struggled to put any weight on my left foot. I withdrew from the rest of the competition.

I left on crutches. I remember watching my father walk away in disgust. I'm not sure if that was the reality, but it was my reality. In my mind, I had failed him and crushed his dreams for me. Still, silently, I was relieved. The pressure had become too much, and my passion for the sport was gone. I was on the brink of a chance to do what I had always wanted, and it now was all over. And yet I felt a sense of relief.

My parents were intent on finding a doctor to help get me back on the ice as soon as possible. I would miss this round of regional and sectional competition, but there was talk of applying for a bye to Nationals as well as a junior international competition in Italy.

I went to see a doctor in Boston. He said the damage was severe due to the cortisone shot. I needed surgery, and he wouldn't know how extensive the damage was until he looked inside. After a six-hour procedure, the surgeon emerged from the operating room to tell my mother that it was amazing that her daughter had been able to walk, let alone skate for the past few months. The damage was that bad. He had to perform reconstructive surgery on my ankle. He informed my parents that I would never be able to skate at a high level again. My skating career really was over. This was probably the most devastating and freeing thing I had ever heard.

sanskrit prayer

Look to this day, for it is life, the very life of life. In its brief course lies all the realities and verities of existence, the bliss of growth, the splendor of action, the glory of power. For yesterday is but a dream, and tomorrow is only a vision. But today, well lived, makes every yesterday a dream of happiness and every tomorrow a vision of hope. Look well, therefore, to this day.

three

KRISTIN AND DAD:
THE PERSON WHOSE
APPROVAL I NEEDED MOST.

THE BELL KIDS 1987

WITH DAD AND MOM

3

LOST: WHO IS KRISTIN WITHOUT SKATING?

I arrived home wearing a cast up to my knee and with absolutely no sense of identity. I was no longer Kristin the skater, the special one, the Olympic hopeful. Suddenly and abruptly, I was just Kristin, a nobody. I had put all my eggs in one basket and the basket broke, spilling out my entire sense of identity and self-worth. As far as structure and activity go, I went from a full schedule to empty, purposeless days.

My parents didn't know this Kristin any more than I did. After all, I had been gone for three years, from seventh through ninth grade, and now I was back living in my family's home. I was a young woman used to being on my own, not the compliant pre-teen girl they had waved goodbye to in Atlanta. While my parents wanted to help me adjust, they had no idea how to facilitate that process. To make matters worse, I was seething with anger. While I had begged my parents to help me follow my dream, I was angry at them for sending me away. I felt profoundly abandoned and misunderstood, with no one to turn to but myself. What now?

One of my dad's favorite mantras haunted me: You are what you do. With a child's naiveté, I had believed I could be at the top of my field as long as I chose to be. With the best of intentions, my father had fed a dangerous illusion. I had believed him when he told me I would win Nationals and go to the Olympics. My whole life was designed for stardom.

My father's hopes and dreams had been crushed, and my house of cards had fallen down. Somehow, we would try to put it all back together. But it got messy. Along with my skating career, I had lost my place as my father's #1. I had fallen off that podium as well. This crushed me.

I was 15 and quickly developed a new obsession, like I did at the Moses,' to control my weight. I refused to eat most foods and stayed in my room for hours on end, exercising and counting calories. This was the only way I felt in control of myself now, and no one was able to convince me to behave otherwise. One day my father tried to make me eat a peanut butter sandwich. He was enraged when I refused. This behavior was an about-face from the pliable little girl who had always marched to his orders. But I had a compulsion to be in control of my own life, and I didn't care about what that meant for others.

I kept losing weight, seemingly in an effort to become less and less of me, matching my outsides to the feelings I had inside. I wanted to hide, become invisible. I did not want to be where I was, but I didn't want to be anywhere else either. I wanted to fade away, and yet I still wanted so badly to be seen. I felt sad and alone and sorry for myself. I had no friends, and my siblings were carrying on with their own activities. I was clearly the family misfit—or so I felt.

My lack of eating and weight loss concerned my parents, which only made me want to lose more weight and eat less. My struggle to be in control made my parents even more frustrated and angry. As a result, my dad became distant and removed from my life. My mother took me to the doctor.

I weighed in at 108 pounds, not too abnormal for a female at 5´4˝. The doctor asked my mother about my behavior patterns and personality. Listening to her answers, I realized she had no idea of what was going on inside of me. The doctor asked if I was a perfectionist, and she laughed, saying, "No." I wanted so badly to be perfect that my mother might as well have said that I was a failure. The doctor recommended I gain a few pounds, but didn't identify a reason to diagnose me as anything but normal.

I struggled in my relationship with my mother, but I also wanted to please her and make her happy. I saw how hard she worked to care for my brother, Ryan, as well as how poorly my dad treated her. During my skating career, I had believed I could and should shoulder all the burdens in my family. Now, I just felt helpless, angry, and a desperate need to stay in control.

My parents reminded me of all they had sacrificed to allow me to follow my dream. I was told I was ungrateful and a spoiled brat (partly true!). My eating disorder was a reflection on them and had to be stopped. Otherwise, they were failing and that was unacceptable.

My mother hired a tutor to get me back up to speed with my education to prepare for the second semester of my freshman year at a nearby Catholic high school. As a new student, I tried to integrate and fit in, and I even had a glimpse of being a "normal" teenager. During the summer at the end of that semester, I joined the local community theatre with some girls I had met in school. I started to enjoy life in a new way. I was having some fun.

It was also now OK to go out with boys. Early in sophomore year in high school, a boy named John asked me to his formal dance. He told me that we would go as friends in a group. John picked me up, shook my father's hand, and promised to have me home safe and sound by my curfew. When I got into the car, John and his friends told me that we would be going to a party instead of the dance. Trying to impress John at the party, I drank my first beer. It tasted terrible, but I liked the way I began to feel—relaxed and comfortable. I fit in. Finally.

John dropped me off without coming to the door. My dad immediately noticed my altered state and asked me what they had served at the dance, "Pretzels and potato chips." I slurred.

He questioned me, yelling, "Where were you and who were you with?" He took out the phone book, threatening to call John's parents. I begged him not to. I was crying as my father told me that he never expected this from me. I had fallen again. I was grounded.

Meanwhile, I had let go of some control around my weight, trying to eat "normally." I was eating cookies, ice cream, and pizza while hanging out with friends—foods I was never allowed to eat while skating. This was a new freedom.

One day, my pants felt a little tight so I stepped on the scale. I vividly remember those pants and that scale in my parents' bathroom. I weighed 127 pounds. I had gained 18 pounds since my mother had taken me to the doctor just a few months before. I immediately panicked and felt out of control again. My body was failing me. Soon after, a friend introduced me to cigarettes, telling me that smoking could help me lose weight. I was hooked.

Out to dinner one night with friends, I went to the bathroom with one of the girls. I mentioned how full I was and how I wished I could get rid of the food I had eaten. She told me that she sometimes made herself throw up when she overate or drank too much. I thought this was my answer. I could eat and stay thin this way. Once I learned this trick, I began to use it often, along with exercise, to control my weight. I would binge and purge in an effort to gain back control of my weight. But I was out of control.

By my sophomore year, I was ready to try some new hobbies to replace skating. I tried running cross country, but several girls were faster than me and it was too much work. I remember my dad coming out for one of my meets and cheering me on. I felt his disappointment. I was not one of the top runners and got very little attention from the coach or my dad. I quit.

I went out for a part in the school play. My dad had returned to his pep talks, so I tried out for the lead. I was called back for another audition, but the part was given to another girl. Once again, I quit.

I tried out for the cheerleading squad. All of my friends made the team. Not me. If I was defined by what I was now doing, I was a failure. I just couldn't find my place to fit in.

So I would find a less healthy way to fit in. My best friend and I planned to drink before going to the high school Halloween dance that year. I had only drank beer that one time before, but I recalled how it made me feel and was excited. I bought a Big Gulp filled with Diet Coke, poured half out, and replaced it with something from the back of my parent's liquor cabinet. I drank this concoction on the way to the dance and quickly began to feel its effects. By the time we arrived, my head was spinning. My friend took me to the bathroom where we ran into the principal, Sister Joan. I proceeded to get sick all over her.

Welcome to the world of alcohol, Miss Olympia!

Because my parents were unreachable, my mother's friend had to pick me up from the dance. She had to stop a few times on the way home for me to get sick. The following morning, I had no recollection of what had happened the night before, but I knew I was in big trouble. My mother explained that I needed to apologize to several people for my behavior and actions, beginning with my father who was extremely disappointed and enraged. He told me I was a disgrace to the family name and threw my skates across their bedroom while I curled up in a ball crying on the floor. My father was disgusted at what I did, which I translated, in my mind, into who I was. I was disgusting, so I believed.

Ironically (or tragically), I had worn a skating costume to the Halloween dance. Why did I masquerade as a skater? Why did I drink that horrible concoction? Looking back, it was all in an effort to escape who I was and who I wasn't. It was as if I wanted to break out of my past persona. Killing the skater with alcohol. She was dead, but who would Kristin be? What would I become?

After this incident, I was more lost than ever before. I felt alone, embarrassed, and humiliated by my actions. I felt immense guilt and shame. I hated myself. I had made a fool out of myself in front of all of my peers and in front of a boy I really liked. I went back to school feeling like a fraud. I'd had a reputation as a good girl, the local ice skating star. That identity was taking a 360-degree turn.

During my junior year, at the same Halloween dance, wearing a different costume, I gave a repeat performance. I got drunk and was caught again. This time I was brought before a disciplinary board with my parents present. The board was concerned I had a problem with alcohol. My parents let them know that alcohol was not the problem, but that I suffered from an eating disorder, which they were taking care of.

My parents were ashamed of me and wanted to sweep my problems under the rug. The more they wanted my problems to disappear, the more out of control I became. My smoking, drinking, and eating patterns worsened. I used diet pills and laxatives. I struggled in school with my grades, at home with family members, and socially. I lived in extreme escapism. Each of my vices served to alleviate the pain, at least temporarily, of living in my body and at home. I did not care about myself and I believed no one else cared for me either.

I frequently drank and drove. One night, I drove to a friend's family house in Princeton, New Jersey. We arrived at the house with a plan to go to a Princeton fraternity party that night. We opened a bottle of the family's homemade red wine and drank it, but it tasted terrible.

On our way, listening to UB40 sing, "Red, Red Wine…" I drove us off an embankment, over a guide wire, just missing a telephone pole, and into a ditch. I had no choice but to confess to my parents, but I still didn't tell them the truth. I told them that I swerved to avoid hitting a deer, a plausible story. I was grounded for another month and had to pay for the repairs myself. But no lesson learned.

In my family, drinking to excess was part of the environment, and I didn't realize that this wasn't true for all families. Both my parents drank a lot, and I never gave it much thought. I also thought that fighting, yelling, and verbal abuse happened in all families. I often coped with our family chaos by binging at dinner and then purging right after. This was a means of controlling the uncontrollable around me. Meanwhile, my father kept coming home drunk, and my mother kept refilling that wine glass she kept in a corner on the kitchen counter.

I later learned that both of my grandfathers, as well as some uncles and other family members, were alcoholics. The problem was out there, but no one discussed it. So when I began to exhibit signs that alcohol and I didn't mix well, my parents did not address it. Too many other things were going on, and, besides, addressing my problem would have revealed their own issues with alcohol.

We were a family with secrets, and it was important to put on a successful show to those outside the family. Any negative or unwanted feelings were discouraged. We needed to stay in line, do as expected, and remain "happy" to look good to the outside world. This is why my father went into such a rage the day after my first Halloween dance performance in 10th grade. He was furious that I had embarrassed the family, not worried that I might have a problem.

Partially because my bulimia was getting worse and more noticeable, my parents decided to drag the whole family to weekly group therapy sessions. The goal was to work together on having me back in the family after my return from skating. But my siblings resented me, and I felt like I was getting in everyone's way. I didn't just *have* a problem, I *was* the problem. I was taking everyone away from their lives to deal with mine. No one wanted any part of it, especially me. Again, I was the lightning rod of the family—all the focus was on what I had done to ruin everyone's life since I had come back into the family. And they were right.

At therapy, I remember my family talking about the impact my behavior had on them. My brother was angry that the ice cream was gone; my sister mentioned how she would bang on the bathroom door begging me to stop throwing up; and my mother voiced disgust with my overall selfish and entitled attitude as well as my disregard for any rules they attempted to set. My father's silence felt like a knife piercing through my heart. I filled in his blanks with disgust and disappointment for the person or lack thereof that I had become. His investment had yielded a negative return. I felt blamed and unfairly wronged. It felt like my family's fingers were pointing at me, but I was refusing any responsibility at this point. The therapy didn't work. I hated being back in the family. But, the truth is, I hated being anywhere.

My parents forced me to continue individual therapy, but nothing really changed. I had my coping mechanisms in place and, to some degree, they were working for me. My grades were poor, and my SAT scores were not great. Skating was in the past, and my future options were looking bleak. My mother and her sister (my Aunt Gail) decided that an all-girls college would be best for me. No distractions and less of a chance for me to get into trouble. I got into Simmons College and that was that. I was heading to Boston to experience a new life, leaving my ugly past behind. Things would be different, I thought.

Unfortunately, although I changed locations, I didn't change inside. In college, life became an even bigger struggle. I would binge to fill the inner void and then purge in an effort to get rid of the hurt, shame, and self-loathing. I drank even more alcohol in college; and the mix of drinking, drugs, smoking, binging, and purging worked together to numb and placate my inner feelings.

I had no sense of self—or my place in the world. I was lost. I didn't care. I had no focus, no real reason to be here ... I was floating through life with no real direction. I was living outside of myself. Beating myself up day after day. I was on the loose at fraternity parties and college bars, seeking love and approval anywhere I could get it. I knew I was in trouble, but I didn't know what to do. I was killing myself by living a reckless, self-abusive lifestyle.

By my sophomore year in college, I had entered into an unhealthy relationship with a guy. At the time, I thought he was everything I could hope for in a relationship. Paul was dangerous, intense, and we had a deep level of connection. Five years older than I, Paul was a part-time painter with no real direction or life goals except to spend time with me. He made me feel beautiful and sexy, and I could not get enough of him. He worshipped me in a way that reminded me of how I felt with my dad when I was skating. This was love, right?

That summer, knowing I was unable to control myself and my various vices, I entered a treatment program, with my mother's help. I decided on a hospital in Boston so I could take advantage of its ongoing support when I was back in school. Out of embarrassment, I didn't tell many friends.

My hospital experience merely began to scratch the surface of what would eventually take years to undo. Over time, I would learn that my self-harming practices formed a protective outer layer designed to protect myself from the pain and hurt inside. I had to learn from the doctors and counselors that my methods of weight loss and control were not working—rather, they were keeping me prisoner in my own body. I was trapped in a self-destructive storm with no shelter.

My time in the hospital helped me start to see that eating all foods in appropriate portions at normal meal times could work to regulate my weight. We were monitored to eat a balanced meal that included dessert. We were not given a choice. It was part of the retraining of the mind and body to see that food was not the enemy. We were also allowed no exercise beyond walking short distances. This sort of strict schedule was reminiscent of my skating days, structured and managed by others.

I recall a woman in her 40s who was so thin that she needed to be hooked up to an IV. The rest of us in the program were in our early 20s. This woman told the rest of us to do what we could now to change so that we would not end up like her. I remember thinking there was no way I would let myself end up there. I planned to walk out of the hospital and be done with this problem.

Of course, that one hospital stay did not cure me. I would be in and out of my binge/purge cycle for some time. It would take years for me to accept myself and my frailties and see myself as someone with challenges, imperfections, and shortcomings just like everyone else.

A few months out of the program, I was back with my boyfriend, Paul, and had jumped back into my old patterns. I decided to attend a support group meeting near my college. A woman spoke about how she was able to stop eating the whole bag of cookies and now could enjoy a couple of cookies and stop. This struck me as unimaginable. But I knew it was something I wanted to be able to do in my life. At that moment, however, I could not visualize a roadmap to get me there.

This woman's sharing helped me more than she would ever know. She had given me the most important gift I could receive—hope. Even though I was still struggling with my relationship to food, I realized that I wanted to someday help others to overcome their own obstacles with food. That was the ray of light that would set me on a path to discover my passion to help others become healthy. This woman gave me a gift—an example of serving others rather than self. This was a new focus where my healing would begin.

As all this was going on, I was in my junior year in college. As part of my communications major, I took a journalism course that year. My professor told me that I had a talent for writing and asked me to write for the school paper. I also started working as a tour guide for the admissions office. I was finally starting to put my best foot forward and give my college experience a try. I was awakening within.

I became friendly with a girl in my class who didn't drink or smoke and was interested in doing well in school instead of partying. Sharon was my first healthy friend, and she represented a positive shift. We began working on the school paper and spending more time together.

I also ended my relationship with Paul. He had been in a serious drug-related car accident, so I had gone to visit him at his home in Connecticut. When I saw Paul's injuries from the accident, I saw him in a different light. I saw Paul's deformities on the inside. I felt uncomfortable and unsafe in his home. His father was drinking beer at 10 a.m, his mother was despondent, and Paul was different toward me. He was needy and yet forceful.

I realized that this relationship was not healthy, and that I didn't belong here. Another crack of light had peeked through the blinds. Paul and I were done.

One of the assignments for my school paper was to write about study abroad programs available for students. While I had no interest in traveling abroad, my interest was sparked by a semester program in Washington, D.C. Not only could I spend a semester in the nation's capital and study in the journalism program at American University, I could have a coed college experience. That spring I was accepted to the Washington Semester Program. This gave me another notch of self-confidence.

Part of the program was landing an internship related to my area of study. Thanks to some family connections in Washington, I worked for the Republican Senatorial Committee. This was during the 1988 presidential campaign, and it was fun to be in the middle of it all. I enjoyed the excitement and energy that Washington offered.

One day while waiting for the shuttle to the American University main campus, I lit up a cigarette. A guy also waiting asked why I smoked. I was quick to answer, "Because I want to." He followed up telling me that I should quit and it would eventually kill me. I responded, telling him, "No one can tell me what I can or cannot do."

I learned that the guy's name was Pat and that he had an internship at the White House. We debated back and forth about smoking. He told me about his grandfather who had died from emphysema, and I shared that mine had too. I ended by saying that I would quit when I wanted to do so and not sooner. Pat shared that he would never date someone who smoked.

Hah! I liked the challenge. Game on. Next we debated the legitimacy of all-women's colleges. I liked his fight. I was intrigued. He was a nice guy, and I enjoyed having a discussion with him. This was unusual for me. While guys usually made me nervous and self-conscious unless I was drinking, there was something about Pat that made me comfortable.

When I went to a bar for happy hour with friends from my dorm one night, Pat happened to be there. He announced to the group that he had one extra ticket for any willing participant to join the send-off at the Vice President's mansion for Vice President George H.W. Bush's presidental debate. I quickly shot up my hand from the opposite end of the table saying, "I'll go!"

It was official; I would accompany Pat to the VP's house for the debate send-off. Although we stood in the rain, waving our small American flags outside the mansion for all of two minutes as Bush boarded his helicopter, Pat and I would spend the rest of the day together, laughing and sharing our lives with each other. We ended our date going to the 10:30 p.m. Catholic mass on campus. I had found my soul mate.

Let go and Let god

When hurting, This too shall pass.

When overwhelmed, Keep it simple.

When worrying, One Day at a time.

When frustrated, Live and let live.

four

HIGH SCHOOL
GRADUATION

4

DO I DARE HOPE
FOR TRUE LOVE?

Pat and I started out sending off George Bush on a rainy Sunday
morning, waving goodbye to Mr. Bush and saying hello to each
other. Throughout that fall, I wondered where the relationship
would go. I thought and hoped that I knew.

My journal entries from that fall describe excitement, fear,
and uncertainty. Pat and I spent a lot of time together. I wasn't
absolutely sure I was in love, but I had never felt this way about
anyone else. With Pat, I felt happy, proud, warm all over, and
comfortable with myself and him. I was both inspired and scared.

We started running together and going to church on
Sundays. Everything about Pat was healthy, and I liked that
about him. He gave me hope, that same hope I had felt when
the woman at the eating disorder support group shared about
not having to eat the whole box of cookies. I was still a rebel who
believed that I was doing all of the right things, at least on the
outside. Key word: *Doing*. I was ignoring how I felt. I kept looking
outside myself for the answers. Pat was my mirror.

Even as I was enjoying my time with Pat, I felt strange. I was wondering about our future, afraid of getting hurt. I felt like I needed to know what was going to happen with us. Not knowing left me feeling out of control. I wasn't even sure what I wanted. I was afraid of exposure, intimacy. Part of me wanted to be with Pat every second and another part drew back. I knew I loved Pat and was afraid to let it show.

At some point in November, I finally let go and allowed myself to be in love. I still had a fear of being left or forgotten, but I let go. Unfortunately, there were just a few weeks left before the end of the semester. There was so much to get done, and all I wanted to do was see Pat. I was going to miss the hell out of him.

After our three-month romance, Pat and I parted ways to finish our senior years of college. Pat returned to Bradley University in Illinois, and I stayed in Washington to take a class over the break and then work on the Inauguration, volunteering at various events. While this was a whirlwind of excitement and fun, I struggled at being away from Pat. I felt lost and alone without him. My mirror was not there. He had become my focus, my obsession.

During the spring of 1989, I tried to focus on being at school and talk to Pat on Wednesdays and Sundays as we had planned. This only reminded me of the routine I'd had to follow with my parents when I was living in Atlanta, skating. I felt that Pat was in charge of our relationship now, and I would do as he requested to keep us together.

During this uncertain time, I drove myself to escape from my fears and sense of low self-worth through any means. I spent all my time *doing*. I struggled with *being*. Thinking of Pat would give me a highlight in my day, which was otherwise exhausting due to the dread I constantly entertained in my head: dread of the unknown, of not being enough or feeling enough.

I consistently dismissed my feelings and told myself, "Don't get down on yourself. Be happy with you." Therein was the heart of my struggle ... to be happy with me. As much as I wanted to be happy, I mostly felt sad and depressed, hollow. A strong army of self-destruction was fighting a weak army of self-assuredness.

My habit of pushing myself through whatever task was in front of me gave the illusion of being a hard worker, dedicated and disciplined, yet I didn't have any means of knowing when enough was enough. I had no internal balance sheet to work from. This entry in my journal, from January 1989, highlights the battle inside me:

> *I have been working so hard on this school*
> *project. I am done. I don't feel happy with myself.*
> *I don't want to stress upon this because I don't*
> *want to feel it. I am always running ... food is still*
> *a tough thing. It brings me down. I can't let my*
> *self-image go down–I'm a great kid!*

There was a disconnect between my body and my mind. I kept letting myself down. I was failing me by depending on me. I needed something else, and for now it would be Pat. But with Pat in another state, I was again at a loss.

Pat and I both graduated from college that spring. My parents surprised me by flying Pat out from Chicago for my graduation party. It was the best present! But then it was time to move on, get jobs and start a life—in different locations. Pat and I would continue our long-distance relationship for the time being.

I lived in D.C. after graduation and got my first job, as a meeting planner at an association downtown. The job wasn't a good fit for me, but I did what the job required and put my all into it. After a few weeks, my boss left and I was promoted to her position. I thought I had arrived. I had my own office and my own assistant now. The thought of all of this was exciting, but the actual structured workday and bureaucracy bored and frustrated me.

Pat and I had our long-distance phone conversations, and I tried to live my life, but I didn't feel grounded. I didn't like myself much, and I longed for Pat and his affirmation. I needed Pat to convince me that I was enough. After Pat's visits, I would feel empty and sad, feeling the drive to keep busy so that I could ignore my feelings.

Pat visited, but each time he left, feelings and fears of abandonment rose to the surface. It didn't matter that Pat wasn't really abandoning me—because my life had been bruised by so many experiences of abandonment: Dad leaving after a fight with Mom, my parents letting me go away to skate, dad leaving me emotionally when I stopped skating, and mom detaching because she didn't know what to do and didn't have the energy to deal with me. The child inside me believed that if I had only been enough or done enough, then they would have kept me. I couldn't help but fear that Pat would leave me too.

I kept trying and trying to be enough, all the while doing whatever I could to escape the fear and pain I didn't want to feel. I needed to protect myself from my own feelings. My old coping skills of using food re-emerged. I went out to the bars and away to the beach with friends on the weekends to party and drink excessively in an effort to dull my fears.

In early 1990, when I was 23, I started seeing a therapist, at my doctor's recommendation. I felt ashamed that I was still struggling with my eating disorder, believing I should have conquered it by now. Why couldn't I stop hurting myself, my body?

The truth is that my feeling of not being enough and punishing myself had never gone away. I had learned to push through any pain and put a smile on my face so that the world thought that I was okay, better than okay. But I was not. I was back in that black hole of feeling the inadequacy and self-loathing that I had felt for so many years. Mary, my new therapist, served as both a looking glass and mirror to help me begin to see myself on the inside. The outer layer of my onion began to be peeled away.

Every Monday at lunchtime, I left work to sit and cry as I shared with Mary the havoc that I was re-creating in my life. I was beginning to uncover the past hurts and experiences that had shaped how I saw myself.

The dysfunction of my family and the disease of alcoholism in both my parents were exposed. I discovered, at least cognitively, that I was not the sole problem in our family. We were all affected by the abuse that was part of our family norm. I had spent years pushing the pain deep down inside and keeping a smile on my face, always struggling to feel better.

Early on, Mary asked me to walk her through my story. She wanted to know about my experience in the hospital and how I had been coping since I was discharged.

My coping mechanism suddenly became clear. I had moved on—insisting that my past issues were resolved—but they weren't. I had been living in a perpetual blackout of survival—escaping in every corner of my life: eating, binging, smoking, and drinking to excess. I did not want to revisit where I had been while in the hospital. I feared that if I allowed myself to feel the pain and the struggle, I would get stuck there. The truth is, I needed to look and feel the pain in order to heal from it, but I was not ready to go there yet. It was much easier to keep putting the daily fires out.

I was getting through each day, not living it. My visits to Mary were like exhaling after having held my breath for as long as possible. With Mary, I shared the ugly, desperate self that I kept carefully hidden from the outside world. I began to learn about Kristin. The pain would keep re-emerging for years, while I was unwilling to let go of the coping mechanisms that kept me from moving on and letting go.

I was desperate to keep my focus away from the past. Pat and our future together were my reasons for living. They gave me the will to keep going but did not help me to live in the present. I needed something or someone to fill my inner black hole. I was dependent on an outside force, not on myself and not on God. For now it was Pat. He would be my life preserver. He would pull me to shore.

One day, a friend suggested we join a new gym opening near my work. I started taking aerobics classes at the Holiday Spa and loved the excitement, energy and of course, the endorphins, that came with it. I was quickly hooked.

Soon after I joined the gym, another friend who taught the class suggested I teach. Me? Teach an exercise class? I thought she was crazy, but I was pleased she thought I could do it. Since no certification was required, my friend taught me some routines.

I would go home after work and practice, often still smoking at the same time. I began to feel that same sense of purpose and discipline that I had felt while skating.

I gave my first class as a substitute teacher to a packed house of members. Because they were expecting the usual instructor, the pressure was on. I was scared that I would not meet their expectations, but I was determined to put all of me out there and do my best. Loud music, strobe lights: I was on stage again, and a familiar feeling of fear and excitement filled my insides. I rose to the occasion and received positive feedback. I was wanted. I was approved of by others. I was good at something. I craved this feeling and wanted more.

From that point on, most of my free time was spent on my newfound hobby. I earned my group fitness certification and began teaching at other facilities during my lunch hour and after work. It felt great to be on a positive path to taking care of myself. Smoking became harder to fit in as it was, of course, affecting my lung capacity.

Pat was pleased with my new interest and supported me from afar. He was busy with his reporting career for a small newspaper in Illinois. I shared very little about my inner struggles because I wanted Pat to move to D.C. to be with me. I hid my anxieties and imperfections behind the miles between us in order to keep him interested in me.

On one of Pat's visits, I tried to cover up what seemed to me a giant ugly pimple on my face. I kept covering the pimple with my hand in an effort to hide it from him. At one point, Pat moved my hand away and told me that he loved me, and that any flaw was a part of the person he loved. While I desperately needed this kind of love, I didn't find it easy to believe. Some part of me kept thinking all love is conditional, and that Pat would abandon me if he really knew me.

I clung to my relationship with Pat and my hope for our future together. But I also turned to exercise as a way to feel solace, as well as a way to escape. When I exercised, I would be able to transcend inner discomfort and pain and feel a temporary lift in my mood. I could feel a sense of control over my body, a power and elation as well as a release. I liked the sense of accomplishment once a workout was completed. I liked how my body felt as I was getting fit, and I knew what to do to get there.

Once I began a routine of exercising and teaching classes, I felt a familiar sense of separateness from myself. My body, once again, could carry me to a level of self-worth that I had only felt in my skating days. I had felt more positive about myself, like I was enough, when performing and winning. I viewed my body as a machine that would do as I asked, as I needed. Now, exercise was giving me that platform to be seen after feeling invisible for a long time. I was back in the performance/approval cycle.

I quickly began to have a following of clients and expanded my class reach, teaching at corporations and facilities all over Washington, D.C. I loved the fitness industry and how I felt when I taught classes. A new drive and passion to help motivate and inspire others emerged. How wonderful to have something to offer the world. I had a place to belong and people with whom to share my passion.

I really wanted to work full-time in the industry, but that would mean a major pay cut, not to mention that I wouldn't be using my college education in journalism. I worried about my dad's disappointment in me. I was frightened to follow this path of internal drive versus the one of power, money, and expectations. Pat, however, supported my passion and my drive to pursue my fitness career.

While pursing my interest in fitness, I continued my campaign to get Pat to move to D.C. and finally succeeded in 1991. Given the huge disparity between housing pricing in Illinois and D.C., Pat had said he would consider moving if I found a place for him to live that was comparable to what he was paying in Illinois ($150 a month for the bottom level of a residential house). I found him a basement room in a small apartment in Bethesda, Maryland with a group of three girls I had become acquainted with through a fitness class. My only concern was that Pat would be living near me.

My expectations of how we would emerge from our long-distance relationship were very different from Pat's. He wanted to make his own way in D.C. while I wanted him to be with me and me only. It was a challenging transition for us. Pat was meeting new friends at his job, and girls were interested in him. My suffocating jealousy over this almost ended our relationship.

My work with Mary helped me navigate this uneasy time and begin to realize that Pat loved me. I began to understand that I needed to learn to trust him, even though it felt impossible because of my past. Mary told me how fortunate I was to have Pat in my life and how unusual it was for someone with my background to find a partner who gave me unconditional acceptance and love. I still fought it. And because I didn't feel worthy of Pat's love, I attempted to push him away repeatedly. I'm so grateful he stayed.

Pat and I were married in 1993, and we built a townhome in an up-and-coming community in Reston, Virgina. We were so excited to move to a new area and begin our life together. I began teaching aerobics classes at a new local gym and got a new job in public relations for an association, working close to our new home. Pat worked downtown and also decided to pursue a master's degree, which took up his weekends.

At work one day, I told the CEO that I loved working in fitness and my dream job would be with Reebok. He encouraged me to pursue my dream and keep him posted. About six months later, I landed a job with Reebok as a fitness representative. The job was not as glamorous as I had hoped or expected, and it came with a pay cut, but I enjoyed the excitement of being part of an international company.

I was working "in the field"—counting how many people at gyms wore Reebok shoes, doing marketing at local fitness events, and selling product into the gyms. The job lasted nine months before Reebok did away with my program and I was let go. I was devastated. No matter that the closing of the program had nothing to do with me, I felt disapproval and rejection. All the old messages came rushing back: I wasn't important enough. I was cast aside and abandoned.

While working for Reebok, I met several fitness professionals. Roger, one of the Reebok fitness pros, asked me to teach in his studio. He wanted me to try out a new class the studio would be rolling out on the east coast. His gym would be one of the first to offer the program: spinning.

I was not particularly excited about riding a bike, but Roger promised that spinning would be one of the best workouts I would ever get. I decided to give it a try—and yes, it was the most challenging workout I had ever done. I loved the experience and wanted more. I agreed to go through the training regimen required to teach. Since I was out of a job, the timing was perfect. I was one of the chosen few, and I was all in.

It was intense, fun, competitive, and exciting to be a part of something new and different. I was on the cutting edge of something big in the fitness world. There were four or five of us instructors, so we spent time together learning and training. One of the male instructors, Sam, was a body builder and personal trainer. One day he invited me to a gym where he trained clients to work out with weights.

I had never really done strength-training workouts, but I was open to learning. Sam was knowledgeable, but more importantly, he said the magic words to me. "You have a great body, and you are a natural." I felt noticed. I had a gift, and it was my body. The one thing I was trying to control—my body—was working, and I was getting approval. Between my new cycle training and then lifting weights, my body started to change and I craved more.

As my focus on changing my body became more intense, Pat was working full time and getting his master's degree. This schedule gave us little time together. Although Pat loved me unconditionally, I had a deep-seated need to be continually reassured of this. I needed Pat to express his love more than was realistic in our busy schedules.

I couldn't put my finger on what was missing in our relationship, so I blamed Pat. If only he were different, I would be happy. I needed more external love and approval than any one human could give. I was like a sieve that couldn't contain approval and love. I couldn't see that I needed to find it within. Our relationship was at a challenging standstill.

I began working with Sam almost daily. I would go with him to the gym after our cycle training, and he would teach me how to lift weights. I would watch him train other women and learn as he urged them to embrace the challenge in order to change their bodies. He suggested that I would be a good trainer for women and could help others achieve results like I had seen and encouraged me to get into personal training. This sense of purpose was intoxicating—plus it gave me an excuse to keep pushing my own body.

As I followed Sam's guidance, my body was changing dramatically. I had a very low percentage of body fat and muscle definition. Getting stronger and faster, I was driven by this metamorphosis. I was in charge of my body and someone, again, believed in me when I'd had no belief in myself. I wanted more. I wanted to be the best and get the recognition that comes with that.

Sam suggested that I get into fitness competition and begin an even more serious training regimen. This felt like a familiar path, one that I wanted to take. I wanted to prove that I was the best at something. I was back in the trap of performance fantasy—my old addiction.

All this affected my relationship with Pat. We were both distant and removed as I followed my passion and my trainer. That winter, however, there was a snowstorm that forced us to stay put for almost a week. We were snowed in, which gave us time to talk and be together.

About a month later, I found out I was pregnant with our first child. God had stepped in. Although Pat and I had discussed having a child, we had just started talking about it—and now it was real. I wasn't sure I was ready to be a mom. All of my focus and hard work on my physical appearance was about to change. There would be no fitness competition. Through my training, I had begun to view my body as a physical specimen, a machine (again!) and something I could control. The pregnancy was about to flip everything on its head.

I was still training with Sam, but things had shifted. I had lost his approval and focus on me. Once my (our) dream of competing in fitness was sidelined. I no longer served any purpose for him. I was obsolete, and it felt parallel to what I had experienced with my father after my skating injury. But now I had a gaping internal hole without an external source to fill it.

I continued to look toward exercise as salvation. While pregnant, I continued to train and teach my classes at the same level. I felt good. I struggled with morning sickness in the beginning, but the workouts made me feel better.

I hated the changes that were happening to my body. I tried to ignore them, but I was no longer in control. I was not willing to accept this lack of control and fought it every step of the way. I learned everything I could on pregnancy and exercise and earned a certification specialty in pre- and post-natal exercise. I learned that as long as I did not start any new exercise or take it the next level, I was fine to continue. I would just need to modify as the pregnancy progressed.

I fought the weight gain while making sure that the baby was healthy. People told me that I was tiny, but I felt huge and out of control. I was desperate to hold on to my sense of self, but I was quickly losing "me" as my body changed shape and I realized my life was no longer about me. It was all about the baby now. Exercise was something that kept me feeling like I still mattered. I still needed that outside approval and validation, but everything was not about me anymore. I hated this feeling.

I remember waking up for my early morning schedule feeling nauseous, eating saltines, and going to teach my aerobics class. Staying home was not an option for me, not because there were no substitute instructors, but because teaching gave me what I needed. It made me feel better, even if just for that hour. I was constantly looking for something external to make me feel better. But nothing would sustain that feeling.

Megan Katherine DiDomenico was born on September 28, 1996, healthy and with a smile on her face. We nicknamed her "Smiley," and the name stuck for years. Megan was an amazing addition, and yet I still struggled to embrace the changes that affected me and my relationship with Pat. I went from a self-focused way of life to being totally depended upon by this tiny, fragile human being. I was lost. Thank goodness for Pat.

I continued to work, work out, and live my life as I did before Megan was born. My life was changing, but I was unwilling to change with it. Responding to a desperate internal need, I returned to exercising less than two weeks after giving birth. Who was I without the things I *did*? I was not willing to find that out yet.

As a child, Pat had learned to be kind, nurturing, patient, and loving. I, on the other hand, had learned not to count on others. I had learned that love was as easily taken away as it was given. Relationships in my family were conditional. As long as you did what was expected of you, you were okay. If not, harsh criticism and judgment were quick to follow. My husband's genuine unconditional love for me, our daughter, and our new family continued to feel foreign, something I couldn't let myself fully trust.

The more Pat extended himself and enjoyed time with Megan, the more I retreated and focused on my training and work. Pat was good at this parenting thing, and since I believed I was not, I let Pat be in charge. I deferred to him on big and small decisions of parenting. I took on a childlike role and put Pat in the role of parenting me as well as Megan.

During the central part of each day, I was home arranging play dates, Gymboree, and music classes, but my heart was not in it. I also worked part time for a sports magazine and taught my spinning classes. I went through life acting like the mother and woman I thought I was supposed to be, without any idea of how to be it. I never felt good enough. For Megan's sake, I was relieved that Pat seemed to make up for my shortcomings, but that didn't make me feel better about myself.

Although I read books on parenting, I felt lost and unqualified to be a mom. My own mother had been distant and preoccupied. She was in the house but not present in my life. Growing up, she often asked, "How are things going?" I always said things were fine. She would say, "That's what I want to hear." I sensed no room for error or discomfort. I was expected to declare everything was fine, even if it wasn't.

While visiting my parents with Pat and my new baby, I asked my mother what it had been like to have me move away to live with another family for skating. I was reminded of the time my mother told me that she "closed the blinds on me."

She explained the challenges of raising my brother Ryan along with three other children. Maybe she thought I was better off being raised be another woman? With such a background, I feared what was to come for me as a mother. How could I give to Megan what I hadn't received myself? How could I provide for Megan while still struggling to be okay in my own skin? Not knowing the answer, I threw myself into my fitness activities and career. I worked to take back control. For starters, I began running more.

MEGAN AND KEVIN CHEERING
ME ON FOR THE RUN PORTION
OF A TRIATHALON.

five

WORLD DUATHLON CHAMPIONSHIPS.

MY FIRST TRIATHLON IN 1997. I FOUND MY NEW LOVE.

6 MONTHS AFTER MEGAN WAS BORN, AND RUNNING THE FASTEST 5K OF MY LIFE!

FROM THE LEFT: MY BROTHER RYAN, FAMILY FRIEND MARILYN MADDEN, MY MOTHER, MY SISTER LAUREN, MEGAN, ME, AND MY DAD

5

I WAS STILL SEEKING, EVEN RACING TOWARD, APPROVAL

In the spring of 1995, the year before Megan was born, I ran my first post-college race, finishing a 10K with ease at an 8-minute mile pace. From the classes I was teaching as well a newfound love of running, I was in good shape. Pat, a serious runner himself, told me I had potential to be really good. With the knowledge I could average an 8-minute mile for six miles without training, I imagined what I could do if I took running more seriously.

Now I had a fresh mission, to see how fast and far I could go. I had the drive and determination, and my fitness was improving. I began winning. Pushing myself through and beyond any pain to achieve my goals, I suddenly felt like someone again. I was good at something. Still looking for my father's approval, I tried to share my goals and achievements with him, but my father didn't seem to care. Perhaps he felt burnt out from his caring and disappointment with my skating career. It continually bugged me that my father didn't care, and

I continued to push, using the competition, the only path I knew to regain his support and attention.

Running filled an intense physical and emotional craving. But, as with all cravings, I needed more and more. Running simply became my newest addiction. I rationalized my excessive workouts as "training" by signing up for races in advance. I told myself that training to reach a specific goal justified my excessive workouts.

Mary, by now my longtime therapist, challenged my motives. She asked what I would do if one day I found myself unable to exercise. She gave me a chilling prediction, "Until you stop using workouts as a form of control in your life, nothing will change. Chasing the elusive goal of being the best runner will never give you what you are looking for." While I heard Mary and kept going to my appointments with her, I wasn't willing to change.

I decided to train with the goal to run the Marine Corps Marathon between 3 and 3½ hours, requiring an average of a 7:00–8:00 minutes per mile pace. While this was a lofty goal, it was a manageable pace for me at that time in my "training." I was excited and anxious when my parents decided to come down for the race. I was once again feeling the pressure of others' expectations on me. What if I let them down?

Roughly two weeks before the race, I strained my IT band, a very painful running injury that stems from overuse. I attempted to rest and rehabilitate the injury as best I could, but I was determined to make it to the start-line of the race, and I did. But at mile 21, with only five miles to go, I dropped out of the race because the pain had reached an excruciating level. My parents left without ever seeing me at the finish line where they were waiting.

This experience was reminiscent of my final skating competition, where I was forced to stop in the middle of my program, ending my chances of moving on to Nationals. After all that training and hard work, I had failed myself and my parents again. I was crushed, but even more determined to compete and prove myself.

When Megan was nine months old, I completed my first triathlon. The women's sprint distance and race (½ mile swim, 15-mile bike and a 5k run) was a great entry for me to the sport. I had been running races and teaching spinning classes, so I just needed to add swimming, which I had never done as a sport.

At the beginning of my training, I barely made it across the 25 meters of the pool. Although I questioned my ability, I kept swimming anyway. I enjoyed the challenge and seeing my subsequent progress.

Competing in my first triathlon from start to finish was a thrill—the challenges of the water, freedom on the bike, and comfort of the discomfort of running. Just completing that first triathlon felt like a huge accomplishment. I cried in elation and relief as I crossed the finish line. That old feeling was back.

I soon hired a coach and shifted into another mode. It was as if I was redoing my skating career. Training for competition was something I knew how to do, and I was driven to succeed. My confidence and strength were building—but unfortunately it was building from the outside in.

As much as competing gave me, it also took away. I was depending on outside approval and nurture to achieve my goals. The more positive feedback I got about my abilities, the more I wanted to achieve. I was still looking to fill an internal hole. Competition in running, triathlon and cycling would be it.

My husband supported my adventures and came to all of my races. Often, my training took priority over other family matters.

Four years after my first attempt at the Marine Corps Marathon, I signed up for the race again. Everything went well until the day before the race. Going out for a 2-mile shake-out run, I twisted my ankle by stepping on an acorn.

Having diagnosed a bad sprain, my chiropractor taped my ankle. In response to my questions, he told me that if I thought of myself as a football player who needed to get back in the game, I could play. That's just what I wanted to hear. I was not going to quit this time.

The marathon, held in October 2001, had increased security and an eerie sense of impending doom. As a country, we were mourning the 9/11 attacks and gripped by fear. I set a goal to run past the Pentagon and see the damage, as the roads surrounding it had been closed since the attack. Assuming I made it as far as the Pentagon, I gave myself permission to get off the course at that point.

Pat and I started out together. After only a couple of hundred yards of limp running, I headed back to the starting area, kissing Pat goodbye and crying. I had quit. Again.

Preparing for the run, I had loaded myself with carbs and eaten an energy gel just before the start. Now I was worried: What was my body going to do with all those extra calories? I decided to try again, just make it to the Pentagon. Maybe then I could find Pat and the rest of the group along the way and cheer them on.

Determined now, I picked up my pace and began passing people. Before I knew it, the pain in my ankle had disappeared, and I was running and feeling great. I finished the race in 3 hours 33 minutes, just before my husband came across the finish line.

He couldn't believe I had done the marathon and that I had somehow passed him along the way! I had completed my first marathon and overcome a physical obstacle.

Discovering racing as an adult was a rebirth of sorts—I was once again receiving approval from the outside world, similar to when I was skating. I also built a network of friends and training partners who enjoyed similar events and training regimens. I enjoyed the rush, the adrenaline, and the feeling of pushing my body to its maximum effort. Being in control of my body gave me a sense of being all-powerful and strong. Keeping up with my training and business, while being a mom, however, made me feel anything but in control.

Training, competing, and pushing myself was familiar. I was good at it, whereas I didn't believe I was a good mother. I did not know how to do life with the family at the center. Once I found racing, the old patterns from skating were reborn in another form, and I found a comfortable home. Oftentimes, I felt comfort in what I knew, not necessarily what was good for me.

As a child athlete, I had developed an incredible ability to disconnect and push my body through any kind of pain in order to achieve a result. It didn't matter how I felt, whether my body was hurting, or what was going on outside of my life, I could figure out a way to complete the training session or performance. Once developed, this ability never left.

I recall an off-ice training session when I was 13 years old in which we were taught to picture our body as a piece of bacon, sizzling in a pan, or an ice cream cone, melting in the sun. We were taught to leave our bodies in order to endure and bypass feelings of pain in the body or fear in the mind. It was a sort of brainwashing exercise.

The kind of discipline required from elite athletes is difficult to sustain. With racing, as with competitive skating, I eventually reached a point where I wanted out, when the pressure and constant work sucked the joy out of the sport. Unfortunately, I didn't know how to stop. With each race I was pulled back into the fold. I would tell myself, this is the last time.

For many years I have been aware that exercise for me is more than just a health benefit. Throughout my life, exercise has given many positive benefits: dedication, discipline, persistence, goals, willingness to try things I'm not sure I can do, a venue to overcome fears, a belief that I can achieve a goal, strength, and mental focus. And finally it allowed me to experience death.

Though I had started exercising for fun, soon the drive to push myself further and further had taken over. I tried new forms—running, duathlon, triathlon, hot yoga ... any form and any combination would work. But it had to be intense.

I also thrive on competition. Why? I have an internal fire that drives me to push, challenge myself, and fight harder. For me, this is more than a desire; it is a need. During intense "training," I am able to channel my energy into the present moment and let go of my anxieties and shortcomings. It is as if I change bodies and move into a separate person. I disassociate from self.

Once I discovered exercise as an adult, it became the main priority in my day—a way to self-soothe and keep me feeling in control. Exercise has provided an escape from stress—a positive, but I also used it as an escape from responsibility—a negative. Exercise gave me a job and helped me inspire and help others in their quest for fitness and health. It also helped me keep my weight balanced and my eating disorder in check.

Exercise has been a passion and a gift, yet, as with anything that fed me, I always needed more. The problem was that I was committed to exercise for the wrong reasons. I viewed my body as an entity separate from myself. As long as I could control my body, make it do anything I wanted, I felt in control. In other words, exercise was a drug and an addiction for me. For a long time, I thought the drug was working. I thought exercise was a viable escape.

Our second child, Kevin Patrick, was born October 4, 1999, just a week after his sister's third birthday. Even though I accomplished a lot over the next few years, I remember very little, except that I was in pain. Physically, the pain stemmed from gaining more weight than with my first pregnancy; emotionally, the pain stemmed from feeling out of control. My eating disorder re-emerged in full force, and I suffered from post-partum depression.

I exhausted myself trying to keep everything going: my business, Megan's activities, and household chores. I had more to do, less time to do it, a baby that needed me, and an active 3-year-old. I resisted letting go of my self-focused pursuits in an effort to hang onto my sense of self by a thread. But things kept falling through the cracks. I was still in therapy, and I started on an anti-depressant. I felt dead inside and was trying to keep the smile on the outside. The medicine helped, but I could not stop my self-critical thoughts and hurtful behavior patterns. I was drinking a lot in the evenings, as well as binging and purging.

I continued to build my personal training business and juggle motherhood as best I knew how. We moved to a new single family home in a nice community with lots of young kids. I packed my days with clients, workouts, and kids' activities. From the outside, my life must have seemed happy and full. On the inside, I was struggling with my eating disorder and drinking to the point of blacking out on occasion. These behaviors had become cemented into my life as coping mechanisms. Both my drinking and working out had become a daily balancing act.

In 2003, the year we moved, I experienced some unusual chest pains. Because of a family history of heart disease, I went to see the doctor. After performing an EKG, the doctor sent me straight to the emergency room, believing I was having a heart attack.

As the medical team checked me into the hospital and put me through a series of tests, I was terrified. On the hospital's cardiac floor, my roommate was three times my age. Nurses gave me medicine I didn't understand and served me Jell-O for dinner. I was healthy, an athlete, what was I doing here? Eventually, the doctors concluded my heart rhythm, though unusual, was normal for me. After every imaginable test, they concluded that nothing was wrong with my heart. Phew! I was relieved!

A few months later, after pushing 4-year-old Kevin on his big wheel bike up our cul-de-sac, I noticed my heart fluttering. It subsided, and I came inside and took a sip of a smoothie. The cold liquid felt uncomfortable going down, and the flutter began again; this time it did not stop. Something weird was happening. I began to feel faint and nauseous.

The next morning, when I awoke to teach my spin class, the flutter was still there. The heart rate monitor I used for training showed an erratic heartbeat, going from 80 bpm up to close to 200 and then back down. I drove to the emergency room instead of to my spin class. I was in atrial fibrillation.

My heart rhythm stayed erratic for the next 24 hours, and the doctors decided to use the paddles (cardioverter) to shock my heart back into rhythm. The doctors explained all that could go wrong in the process; namely, the procedure might not work and I could die.

I went into a panic at this news. Afraid to die on that day, I called my father, who'd had surgery due to heart disease a year earlier. Dad and I, however, were not on speaking terms due to a blow-out argument we had while we were visiting my parents' home in New Jersey. My dad had become enraged after a long night of drinking, and we left my parents' home without saying goodbye.

As I lay in the hospital awaiting my fate, my father and I both cried as he told me I would be okay, that he was sorry, and that he loved me. It was amazing how all the anger and grudge-holding went out the window when I was faced with a life-and-death scare. I think it was God's way of getting the relationship back on track.

In the end, the doctors determined that the atrial fibrillation was a fluke and nothing to worry about. I would need regular check-ups, but was free to exercise without restriction. The doctors prescribed a blood thinner on a short-term basis in case of a reoccurrence. I went right back to my strenuous daily exercise schedule.

On a weekend visit to my parents in 2007, my father suggested I investigate my heart condition more fully. Shunning his concerns, I resented his suggesting that I might be at risk. After all, I was competing successfully in triathlon and training to be the best in my age group. My livelihood was exercise and nutrition. I practiced what I preached (except for excessive drinking, binging, and purging!). How dare he?!

My father died the following Tuesday of a massive heart attack. I felt numb. After his surgery, I had watched him return to his self destructive patterns. I tried to share my knowledge about health and fitness with him. I felt betrayed, not important, once again abandoned by him. Why didn't he care enough about us to change his ways? My anger morphed into sadness, which ignited my inner drive to keep working to get his unattainable approval. Now, I swore I would not end up like my dad. I would do everything in my power to eat healthfully and exercise. I had my hidden behaviors, but, as I saw it, I was keeping them in check.

I did eventually go to a cardiac specialist at John Hopkins at the recommendation of my general cardiologist. When the doctor declared I was in no danger of dying from my genetic heart condition, Pat and I left the hospital feeling confident that I was in the clear. I took the news as a green light to continue to compete and challenge my body with vigorous exercise. So I did. The expert had told me what I wanted to hear. I went on to compete in running, biking, and triathlon events over the next seven years, including two Ironman distance triathlons.

The year my dad passed away was the year I competed in my first duathlon, a run-bike-run competition. My coach had encouraged me to give it a try and believed that I could make it to the World Championships, which happened to be nearby in

Richmond, Virginia, that year. I recall the brutal training and long, hard workouts, but I thrived on all of it, just as I had when I worked with Sam. Someone believed in me again, as my dad had for years in my skating. I was more than willing to work hard to recreate the drive to championship that had been halted in skating.

As I competed in a qualifying event, trying to earn a spot in the World Championships, I had an overwhelming feeling of Dad's presence during the 56-mile biking portion of the race. It felt as though Dad was pushing me along and I began crying with joy as I knew he was close. As I crossed the finish line, I had done it; I had achieved what he had believed I could do and made it to the World Championships. The sport was duathlon rather than skating, but for me it counted.

The night before the World Championships duathlon race, I sat in the bathroom of our hotel room, alone and afraid. I called and texted my coach looking for solace and calm ... validation that I could do it. I felt the same pressure and fear I had felt years earlier before a big skating competition. I knew what would be required of me the next day, and I felt a deep sense of fear—a fear of failing to achieve what was expected of me. It was the same fear I had felt as a child—a fear of not living up to others' expectations and a fear of not being enough. What if I failed? Who would I be?

The next day, I ran the race of my life and finished in the top three in my age group, earning a place on the podium. I was elated that I had finally achieved this lifetime goal of being a champion. It wasn't skating, but it counted for me. The hard work, discipline, and sacrifice had paid off. I was finally the winner my father willed me to be. I soon realized that even this accomplishment wasn't enough. I was driven to push harder, to achieve even more.

At my father's funeral in 2007, a priest and family friend shared some words of wisdom with me: Expectations are the cause for human suffering. I would need to suffer and live out this pattern repeatedly and in different venues until I would learn that the constant struggle for approval is elusive and never ending. There is always a need for more.

When I was deciding whether or not to sign up for my second Ironman in 2013, my coach told me I had nothing to prove to anyone. As she counseled me over the phone, I listened for any inflection or comment that would push me in a direction for the decision. I kept vacillating. In so many ways, I was sick of pushing myself and competing. But sport had become a pair of old comfortable slippers I was struggling to give up. It was easier to go with what I knew than try something different. I knew how to train and push my body. So I signed up again.

Although I was an amateur rather than a professional athlete, I could relate to the struggle to stop that many top athletes experience. When you spend a good portion of life working to be something and that is what you know how to do, it is very hard to give up that identity—even when you know it's time. Even now, I am not sure I know how to live another way.

SIX

GETTING ENGAGED:
THE 1992 KENTUCKY
DERBY

THEN ... (ST. LUCIA 1993)

... AND NOW

6

AS WITH MOST THINGS, I JUMPED INTO ALCOHOL WITH BOTH FEET

In high school, after skating ended and my eating disorder started to dominate my life, I also found alcohol. Everyone else was doing it and not only did I want to fit in but I wanted to escape being me. Alcohol did the trick.

In early adulthood, my drinking escalated at times and I would drink too much, but I thought this was just normal. Whether it was too much at a wedding or a party or a concert, I was always the one who had too much and couldn't handle it. I would apologize to my husband or friends for my behavior after these episodes, but nothing changed. I repeated this cycle for years. I spent most of my time either running through life or numbing out to erase it.

On many occasions, I'd wake up having forgotten what had occurred or what I had said the previous night. I'd have to ask Pat to fill in the blanks. When this happened, I would feel deep shame and remorse. This would typically lead to a fresh binge/ purge eating cycle. I would revisit hell in these dark encounters, feeling lost and out of control. I would wake up with a hangover and promise myself that I wouldn't drink again. Then at 6:00 p.m., I would pour myself a glass of wine. And then another.

When I drank in the evenings, my kids had a single parent, my husband. Pat would pick up the slack for me and take care of the kids' needs. He was the source of reliability and dependability for all of us. This was his role. It was as if I was the third child.

I have always been a disciplined person, so I was sure I could stop drinking if I wanted to make that change. According to the Dietary Guidelines for Americans, moderate drinking for an average-sized healthy woman is no more than one drink in any one day. I was confident I could stay within that limit. So I tried. Then I would try to set up control barriers, change my glass size, refill my first glass before it was done, making it a continuation of my first glass. I'd reason that a partial refill wasn't technically a second glass, was it?

I have heard it said: If you need to control your drinking, you have a drinking problem. Control was a big part of why and how I drank as well as why and how I exercised. It was how I lived—feeling in control or out of control. Since my skating days, my life had been in the control of others. I lacked a sense of self and struggled to be in my own skin. That, combined with a family history of addictive patterns, created a need for me to insert external forces of control.

When I drank, I felt a sense of balance in my life, a temporary illusion of relaxation. Drinking wine gave me the calm I could not create on my own. It soothed me and helped me feel on an even keel, like a see-saw with equal weight on either side. I grew to need that glass of wine at the end of my day. It's not so much that I needed to get drunk, although sometimes that would be the result. I needed to drink to escape being in my head. But wine never did fully erase my thoughts and feelings. It would numb things temporarily, which gave me some relief. I yearned to hold on to the numbness for as long as possible.

I tried for years to moderate, stop, limit, and stop again. I hated waking up in the morning with a foggy feeling. Even so, alcohol was my relief, my refuge at the end of the day. It was my light at the end of the tunnel. Wine gave me an ability to turn the light switch off. But for me, there was no dimmer. I was on or I was off. Once I poured my first glass of wine, I was able to move into a different realm. This was my realm of letting go. I let go of responsibility, accountability, productivity, and a sense of living. I felt a calm of sorts, but also a distance from reality.

In so many ways, I have had a great life, but my sense of self-acceptance and true belonging were always missing. I went through the motions of life, as if I were following a path that was not mine, but rather what I thought I was supposed to do. College, job, marriage, kids—this is what was expected of me. But I always had that feeling of something being missing. Wine and my other abusive behaviors had covered me up. Yet I was right there all the time. I avoided looking at myself, my behavior, and my responsibility in things. The drinking covered up my insides, the parts of me I did not like, the parts of me that I had been running from for years. Because it was covered up, it was also impossible for me to see what my own behavior patterns were doing to me.

At least on the surface, I was able to be a mom, wife, business owner, and elite athlete. I spent my days like most people, but my drinking gave me a handicap that I was unwilling to see for a long time. Life was better when I removed the handicaps blocking me from truly living.

There were days when I could have two glasses of wine, but I often kept going beyond any limit I had set for myself. I drank wine in the evening and thought I was managing my drinking well. Many days I tried and failed to set up control barriers that would limit my number of drinks. Little tricks kept me feeling in control, like keeping a little bit of wine in the bottle or switching from white to red so that I would never drink a whole bottle. I believed that exercise, food, and drink would create a structure that would ultimately help me to get through each day. At times, my self-discipline would kick in and help me to regulate my intake of alcohol, but I didn't have a natural desire to limit myself.

Most of the time, I tried to deny I had a problem with alcohol, but the awareness broke through. In a diary entry during a summer break as far back as college, I wrote that I needed to stop drinking, that it "didn't agree with me." I vowed to get support when I returned to college. But it would be years on a rollercoaster of guilt, shame, and remorse before I let go of this heavy yoke.

After my dad passed away, my siblings and I became increasingly concerned about my mother's drinking. It became obvious that she had a problem, and that it was escalating. In one of my therapy sessions, Mary suggested I attend a group meeting for individuals affected by another person's drinking.

Until this point, it had never occurred to me that my parents' drinking habits were abnormal. I only knew what I had witnessed growing up.

In November of 2007, I walked into my first support group for families of alcoholics, unsure about what to expect. I fidgeted in discomfort as I looked around the room. As the meeting continued and people shared, I realized I had inadvertently come to a meeting for alcoholics. I listened as an older man, roughly the age of my dad, shared how his life had changed since he stopped drinking. He was now living a life with real meaning. I felt extreme sadness as I thought about how my dad had passed away without knowing this way of living.

Soon after, I found the correct meeting and the people in that group quickly became a catalyst for change in my life. I heard the stories of others with similar dysfunctional family histories involving alcoholism and addiction. I learned that alcoholism is a family disease that affects each member of the family.

I began to work on myself in a new and loving way. I began to let go of my past and understand that my parents were sick and had done the best they could with the limitations they had. My father and mother had both grown up with alcoholic fathers. I began to understand that my winning an Olympic gold medal would not have changed any of these circumstances. My self-imposed child-hood expectations were both unrealistic and unattainable.

In 2010, a friend invited me to attend a support group for women with a drinking problem. She claimed the meeting would help me understand my parents' disease. I recall looking around the meeting room at a number of beautiful, put-together women. The women in this meeting were not at all what I was expecting. I had shown up in sweat pants and was likely hung over from the night before.

A woman, who looked like a PTA president, shared a story about going out to dinner with her husband. She described watching the server carrying a cold glass of chardonnay on his tray. As the server passed her table, the woman's eyes lingered while she fantasized about how the glass would feel in her hand and how the thin rim would feel touching her lips as the first sip of magic potion went down. I was following along—experiencing the fantasy with this woman. I could taste the magic of that first sip.

I was caught off-guard when the woman shifted the story into thanksgiving that this spell was now broken and she now felt free. The woman could now be completely present with her husband and enjoy their time together without drinking.

It struck me that I couldn't say the same. I needed my wine to enjoy a dinner out with Pat. I could not imagine how I had come to this point. I began to cry as I connected to the story and realized for the first time that I might have a problem. For three years, I had been going to meetings because I understood my parents had a problem—not me! I continued to go to my meetings, but now I struggled with my dawning realizations about myself as well as with coming to grips with my parents' disease.

A wonderful friend and mentor, Kathryn, helped me through my recovery as an adult child of two alcoholics, but I still hadn't begun my own recovery as an alcoholic. I continued to drink and act out. I struggled to be present for my family and juggled my addictions to food, exercise, and alcohol daily. I was engaged in a selfish, self-focused lifestyle that I could not acknowledge was destroying me and my closest relationships.

In the spring of 2011, I decided to do a 21-day cleanse, during which I would have to stop drinking. I figured the cleanse would give me the structure I needed. I was miserable for 18 days, and then we arrived for a visit at Pat's parents. They offered a margarita, and I couldn't bring myself to say "no." I had made it through 18 days after all. I was close enough, right? I deserved it?!

Everything finally came to a head during my daughter's junior year in high school. Megan was struggling with the stress of the SATs, five advanced placement classes, searching for the right college, playing varsity lacrosse, and having a boyfriend. She was acting out while I was doing the same. I began to become aware that I couldn't be the mother Megan needed. I was at the end of my rope and unsure what to do. Pat and I sought professional help to try to figure out how to parent Megan through this.

On March 28, 2014, Pat was out of town. Kevin had fled the scene as he often did. Our home had become a decidedly unwelcoming place. Megan and I were in a rage. I left the house hysterical, unsure of what to do and where to turn. I called my friend, Kathryn, and told her I was scared for my life and my daughter's. I was afraid to leave Megan, but I was also afraid to stay at home. Kathryn told me to come over to her house. I followed her direction.

As we sat at her kitchen table, she asked if I was ready to stop drinking. Huh? Here I was with all this misery, fear, and worry about my daughter, and Kathryn's solution was for me to stop drinking?

I'm not sure where the answer, "yes," came from; perhaps I knew it was the only thing I hadn't tried. Kathryn told me that all I needed was a willingness to be willing and that I had to believe in a higher power—God. She told me to go home, pour any alcohol down the drain, and then get on my knees and ask for help—and to say "thank you" for keeping me from a drink. I woke up the next morning and repeated those prayers and have been doing it ever since.

I began to pray in a new way. It involved a daily, constant connection with a higher power that I call God. I did not learn to pray this way in a church. This was a kinder, gentler relationship with the God of my understanding. He was accessible always. I would learn to depend on Him in a new way, a way that would create a greater sense of internal peace and freedom.

I started by praying to become willing to have those things in my life that were blocking me to be removed. I did not pray for specifics, only His will for me. Sometimes I would just say, "Help me." When I did this, I was admitting that I was not in control and God was. I finally admitted that my strong sense of self-will and discipline could not help me with my drinking problem. Everything I had worked so hard to develop in my life would need to be gradually stripped away. I would need to learn a new way of living.

I would need to bolster my willingness to surrender to this new habit of relying on my higher power by realizing that I could not change my destructive patterns alone. I had to give up control and let go of my struggle. I was learning to let go of the reigns and hand them over to someone who could handle this burden. I was also building a support network of women who were also on a journey to deal with similar patterns. Each of us was working to make a positive change in our lives.

Drinking had become a built-in coping mechanism, a regular part of every day. Quitting was like removing a major appliance from my kitchen that I used every day. I think back to when the microwave broke at our house a few years ago. We decided not to replace it.

At first I would reach for the microwave, but then I'd remember it wasn't an option. Cooking certain foods took planning and alternate methods. Removing alcohol from my daily pattern of life was similar. It was no longer an option, so I had to learn alternatives.

There was a physical loss—missing the glass, the way it looks, the sound of wine being poured, the social aspect, and more. I had grown up around drinking; and it had been an integral part of most social functions, not to mention holidays, birthday celebrations, vacations, sporting events, and the list goes on. Alcohol was everywhere I went.

When I first stopped drinking, the most challenging time of day was just before dinner. I was in the habit of sipping on wine as I prepped the meal. Today, drinking at that time of day rarely crosses my mind. I am grateful for this change, but it took a full year for me to not crave wine with my nightly cooking ritual. Once I put new rituals and patterns in place, a new normal was established in my life.

I remember a day that our family went to a baseball game, and it seemed as though the beer guy was taunting me. He must have gone up and down the aisle where we were seated every other minute. At such moments, I realized how alcohol had served as a major source of entertainment and enjoyment for me. In time, I would learn to be present and enjoy the actual event I was attending.

For a while, I mostly attended alcohol-free events where I could strengthen my sober muscles. It was challenging to get through the holidays—hosting Thanksgiving dinner, Christmas, New Year's Eve—without drinking. Each holiday I made it through sober made me stronger for the next one.

It wasn't until I stopped drinking that I was able to see the impact my drinking had in my life. I began to live with less guilt, and my feelings of shame and insignificance diminished. I was able to be more available and participate in evening activities with my family. I began to feel a new joy and sense of well-being that I had never before felt. I was available and present with my kids, my husband, and friends. My relationships were healing, and I was starting to help other women by sharing my story in safe places. I was healing from the inside. This was a new and joyful way of going through my days, and I wanted to keep it going. God had begun to do for me what I was unable to do for myself. There is still much more work to do.

On the day I quit drinking, sitting at my friend's kitchen table in complete despair and hopelessness brought me to my bottom where I was desperate and willing to try living in a different way. The fear was ever-present, however, of not knowing how to live in this world without my wine. Today, I have tools and support to live without this vice. Along the way, my mother also stopped drinking and today our relationship is improving as we are healing on our own paths.

Since I stopped drinking, in March 2014, life is now a gentler roller coaster ride. On some of the first days after I stopped drinking, I felt the incredible high of being alcohol free. On other days, I missed the relief it gave me. But the highs and lows are becoming less dramatic. The need to control everything has lifted somewhat. I have learned to embrace the positive feelings and new patterns of real joy and realize that the challenging times will eventually pass—with or without a drink. Drinking usually only makes them worse, rarely better. Time and space from my last drink makes it easier to live without it. It is a new normal for me. Life is still challenging in many ways, but I know that drinking will not change that.

I still miss having a glass of wine at times, but for me the benefits of not having alcohol in my life far outweigh the consequences of my prior way of living my life. I had lived like a bull in a china shop, knocking down whoever and whatever got in the way of getting what I wanted. I am now enjoying life experiences without a perpetual fog around me. I am learning who I was meant to be and how to accept myself as I am. Giving up alcohol was the most uncomfortable change I have had to make (next to quitting smoking in 1993), and yet I feel a freedom that I have yearned for my entire life.

my daily prayer

God, I offer myself to Thee — To build with me and to do with me as Thou wilt. Relieve me of the bondage of self, that I may better do Thy will. Take away my difficulties that victory over them my bear witness to those I would help of Thy Power, Thy Love, and Thy Way of life. May I do Thy will always.

THE START OF THE
RACE THAT CHANGED
EVERYTHING.

seven

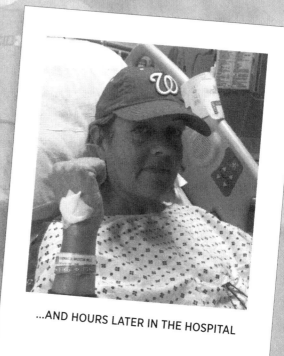

...AND HOURS LATER IN THE HOSPITAL

OLD HABITS ARE HARD TO CHANGE

When I collapsed during that 10-mile race in October 2014, my near-death experience (NDE) was not the classic light-down-a-tunnel vision you see in the movies or on television. The experience was more of a feeling, a sense of relief, a letting go followed by a sense that I was floating while being supported in a comfortable place. I experienced the letting go of my need to direct and control what I could not control—my life.

I recall a struggle to communicate with those around me on the trail. I tried to tell them to get help and do something quick. I was aware that I was unable to speak or communicate in any way to translate my thoughts into words. So I let go.

As my body lay motionless on the trail, I felt as if I had literally let go of this world and ventured to a new place, a different realm. I was being held on a giant pillow. It was unbelievably soft and fluffy, and I recall thinking, "What is this? Where am I?" I had a feeling of physical lightness, which I wanted to bottle and bring with me wherever I happened to go next.

I was not aware that I had passed on or died, nor did I feel any pain or discomfort. I just recall being in a place of complete peace and quiet, a gentle and freeing comfort such as I had never known. In this space, all worry, angst, anger, frustration, self-doubt, and self-criticism had left me. Hurts and old inner wounds were gone, as if an outer shell had been taken off of me and I was free from any suffering.

In the months before this event, I had been working hard to let go of some of the personal struggles and experiences that had been chaining me to my past. This "visit" opened up a connection to a place beyond this realm of struggle.

Then my father appeared and the scene changes. He had died eight years earlier at age 65, but this was not a 65-year-old version of my father before me. He appeared to be a much younger version of himself. We were standing in a corner of a nondescript room, just white with red walls. There was no conversation between us, just a sharing of physical space. Then my father spoke to me: "I love you and I'm worried about you." I did not answer him. There was nothing else spoken between us. No goodbye or "It's not your time yet." That was it.

In the months following my near-death experience, I thought a lot about this encounter. What was my father worried about? And why did I see him?

Dad and I were very close when I was younger. He was my biggest cheerleader during my competitive ice skating days. He showed his love by giving approval for the successes in my life, starting with skating. I always strived to prove to him that I was good enough by "doing." Maybe by his visit, Dad was telling me that I'm enough just as I am. I don't have to do anything to earn his love. He loves me just for being me, not for *doing* anything.

Or maybe my father was warning me: If you don't stop pushing yourself and your body to the extreme, you will die. Maybe he was saying he didn't want me to go through life the way he did—believing he was invincible and not listening to his heart. Dad had always taught me to work hard and persevere. Was he warning me to stop pushing myself? Did I need to hear it from him to really change my ways? I'll never know for sure. "I love you and I'm worried about you" is all he said.

Suddenly, I was being pulled out of the cushioned room with red walls and back into reality. My re-entry felt like being sucked through a vacuum. The emergency room was the complete flip-side from where I had been: Bright lights ... beeping machines ... freezing cold. I didn't want to be there. Returning to consciousness was almost a disappointment. I wanted to stay where I had been. I had been held in the most peaceful comfort you can imagine. I was trying to hold on to all that I was experiencing—the true joy and sense of peaceful comfort.

As I became aware of my surroundings, I felt someone holding my hand. It was my daughter, Megan. I asked her not to let go. "I just saw my dad," I said, and told them about the red walls and the soft pillows that held me.

I was shivering with cold and struggling to warm up. Doctors said this was normal as my body had gone into survival mode when my heart stopped beating—all the blood rushed away from my arms and legs in an attempt to save my organs. I also had some back pain and, like a good personal trainer, asked if anyone had a foam roller I could borrow. That's when Pat says he knew I would be okay.

In the years after my sudden cardiac death, many have asked me to describe my near-death experience. The best way I can describe it? I felt like what I imagine a baby feels like inside her mother's womb—warmth, comfort, no knowledge of past pain or future problems ... at total peace. As I passed over, I felt my struggles, worries, and all discomfort removed from my body. They had evaporated from me. It was a rebirth of sorts ... it was a second chance.

I thought a lot about what had happened and what it meant. Why didn't I die, when other athletes who suffer similar collapses do? I wondered what would have happened if I hadn't slowed down to run with my friend. What if I had decided to finish at the 5-mile mark? So many split-second decisions had put me both me and Dr. Tevar together at just the right time.

Every day, simple twists of fate play a part in our survival, and we never even notice. Maybe we leave the house 30 seconds late for work and miss a traffic accident. On the morning of my NDE, Dr. Tevar almost didn't make it to the starting line. His wife is the one who does the races, and it wasn't until the last minute that the doctor's mother-in-law could come to the house and watch their children, making it possible for both Tevars to run this particular race.

In the days and months after my NDE, I was realizing that God has a plan for me. I wasn't sure what that plan was, except to be there to share my experience, strength, and hope with others. It was clearly not my time to die.

Even so, holding on to that space of peace and complete-ness in love and comfort hasn't been easy. I know the peace is there, not far away. My experience taught me that when I can let go of control, I can be at true peace exactly as I am. This is my ongoing challenge and life work.

Old habits and cravings die hard. I have an addictive personality, and exercise is, by far, my most stubborn addiction. For years, exercise and training had kept me at a distance from myself and those who love and care about me. It acted as a barrier between me and my feelings of self-loathing. My exercise was like a blanket that kept me covered. Without it and what it gives me, I feel my inner hole, an aching sadness, unprotected. After exercising (at the level I want), I feel as if I am wearing a coat of armor and can face anything. Without it I feel vulnerable and weak. I am human. The drive to exercise at high levels is constant and compelling. The urge just never goes away.

As a precaution following my sudden cardiac death, doctors fitted me with an implantable cardioverter defibrillator (ICD) located beneath my skin near my heart. This pocket-watch sized pacemaker device is designed to monitor my heart and shock it back into rhythm should I have another life-threatening episode.

Doctors also gave me a prescription medicine to take before exercise. Even with all this, I soon convinced myself that the episode that nearly killed me was a fluke. Exercise remained a priority in my daily schedule.

I didn't begin to believe there was a limit to what I can do regarding exercise until my heart stopped again on May 17, 2015, a mere seven months after my sudden cardiac arrest (SCA). I was running with the women in my regular Monday evening workout group. It was hotter and more humid than usual that evening. Three minutes in, I had started a slow jog when I felt just a bit off. I checked my heart rate, but the readings seemed normal.

Suddenly, I felt dizzy. I told a client that I was going to walk but would catch up. Then I passed out. My clients watched as my body received the shock, similar to watching someone having a seizure. Luckily, a few of them knew my story and understood that the shock was my ICD doing its job.

As I came back to consciousness, I found myself on the ground, and my head hurt. One of my clients explained that I had fallen and had another episode. She assured me that I was going to be okay. My internal defibrillator had worked and shocked my heart back into rhythm, saving my life.

I couldn't believe my heart had stopped again. I felt terrible for my clients, who were naturally scared by what they had witnessed. I found myself calming a couple of them down as I felt perfectly fine almost immediately. I was pissed off and embarrassed. I had truly believed this would never happen again.

Just to be sure, I went to the hospital and was released that same night. At the hospital, Pat and I learned that my heart rate had jumped from 123 to 300 in a single beat. That is how quickly it happened. It took 30 seconds for the internal defibrillator to restart my heart and re-establish a normal rhythm.

This episode made the seriousness of my heart condition very real. It had been seven months, almost to the day, of my NDE. Now, there was no pretending that first episode was a fluke. There was no denying that my life patterns needed to be substantially changed. I was reminded once again that I am not in control. I can't beat or control this heart condition.

Physically, I had always felt invincible, able to control my body with my will. After this episode, I had a new understanding of my limits. The experience took me off my throne as an accomplished trainer and coach and made me an equal, if not a subordinate to others, in the one area I had always felt I was in control. I was not in control, and now I knew this for sure.

A month after the second episode, we went to Minnesota to visit the top specialist for hypertrophic cardiomyopathy (HCM), the doctor at the forefront of this genetic deformity of the heart. It is a hereditary disease that is hard to test for and difficult to diagnose. I definitely have it. The tricky part is that there is neither rhyme nor reason as to why this happens to me. We only know that, in my case, the malfunction happens during a form of cardiovascular exercise.

I thought I had been following guidelines for heart rate, duration, and intensity during my workouts. None of these factors came into play when my heart malfunctioned again. As months passed between my first and second episode, I had stopped taking the beta blocker medicine doctors had prescribed because I didn't like the effect it was having on my workouts. I couldn't push my body and this felt uncomfortable for me. My initial fear had subsided as the days ticked by. I decided to do things my way, not the doctor's.

The specialist gave me the bad news: No intense athletic training and no competing any longer for me. The experience was eerily familiar—much like the time the orthopaedic doctor told me at age 16 that I would never again skate competitively after my ankle surgery.

I was not going to have the comeback story I had hoped for. I was not going to defy all odds and race another Ironman. My comeback would be one of acceptance and change. It would involve becoming a player for my new coach, God. Even with God's help, however, changing out of known patterns is the most challenging thing we do, even when our life depends on it. I still struggle in this area.

I felt some relief at learning that I could no longer compete, just as I had at age 16. But I was also relieved to learn the shutdown didn't need to be as complete as it had been with skating. I could still exercise—and, hopefully, this would be enough to meet my needs.

MY NEW GOAL: EXERCISING
TO LIVE RATHER THAN LIVING
TO EXERCISE.

eight

THE ONES I LOVE:
MEGAN, KEVIN, AND PAT ...

AND RIGLEY TOO!

GRIEF, ACCEPTANCE, AND FINDING MY WAY

When I talk to friends who are racing or doing three-hour training rides or signing up to do races, I sometimes still feel a loss. Or when friends are going to a winery or a concert or on a party bus where drinking is part of the entertainment, I feel a loss. These parts of me have died. The driven, competitive piece that had defined me for most of my life died, and I still grieve it. My need for relief, comfort and escape using alcohol is no longer a go-to option for me. I am addicted to anything that can give me a sense of relief. Regarding exercise, God keeps telling me the best way to live, and I still try to keep doing it my way.

My addiction to exercise works just like any other addiction. For example, alcoholics delude themselves into believing they can stop themselves after a few drinks. I delude myself into believing I can exercise just a little longer and a little harder. Eventually, all addicts end up needing more, more, and then some more.

It's easier for me to accept the reality of my addiction when it comes to alcohol than when it comes to exercise. Perhaps this is because I am cleared by the doctors to exercise with certain restrictions. No doctor clears me to drink alcohol with some restrictions.

I have gone on and off my medicine in hopes that I can beat this disease. To no avail. I have had a handful of other episodes where my heart went into ventricular tachycardia and my ICD shocked me back into a normal rhythm. The first time I was in disbelief and frustrated but glad the device had worked. The second time, I was pissed—and again the disbelief. How could this happen again? I had been sure it would not happen. The third time, I was sad. And then it happened again. ...

I hate that I have to deal with this disease today and forever. I don't want to change, and yet I feel closer today to accepting my need to change in this area of my life. I am back on my medicine and willing to work out differently. I am not going to claim victory in this area of my life, but I am on a continuum of progress, moving away from those behaviors that do not serve me any longer and moving towards recovery. Every day, I must let go of those barriers that block me from being the best version of myself so that I can become the real me and help others to do the same.

I still use my exercise as a check and balance. It can still give me relief from my internal pain. But I am also learning to sit with the feelings I have always run from. It is an illusion of control that has been challenged a number of times. But I still exercise. The fact is that running and working out relieves my depression. It helps my chemical imbalance. But I've come to accept that exercise is not a cure-all that can heal my internal struggles or help my relationships. It does not change me or even my body that much. I exercise because of how it makes me feel: calm, centered, relaxed, and, yes, when my body feels good, I feel in control. And then God reminds me again that I am not.

One morning in 2018, as I was planning to head out for a bike ride, my dog, Rigley, started nipping at me and jumping up on me. This was strange behavior as she had already had her morning walk.

So what was the problem? She had food. I played with Rigley a little, expecting that she would be consoled and lie down. It didn't happen. I abandoned my bike ride and decided to take her out. We'd had a nice run the day before, so I thought I would run with her now and bike later. Off we went.

Once we got to the trail, Rigley stopped and wanted to go home. What?!?! I refused to listen and pulled her along, coaching her to run with me.

Something in my body didn't feel right. I pulled Rigley back and told her to walk. We walked. And then we started running again. Once more, I slowed to a walk as I felt off. The third time we started, I suddenly knew. It was happening. I'm not sure what I said out loud; was it "help," or "oh no, God." I let go of Rigley's leash and dropped to the ground, feeling dizzy and faint, with my heart rate racing. My defibrillator went off and shocked my heart. I fumbled to call Pat as I was alone in the woods and not sure what was going to happen next.

Once again, I was focused on exercising as much as I could on any given day. Once again, the defibrillator did its job and saved my life. This is my reality. I am not in control. I am reminded when God literally stops me in my tracks.

What can I learn from this experience? I still hate this disease and wish it would go away forever. I wish that my will-power and push-through way of life worked. But it doesn't. This disease is not something I can beat. God knows I have tried. Really! Part of me still thinks I know best and I can figure it out. I am shown repeatedly that is not true.

Dog spelled backward is God. God shows up for us in amazing ways. He challenges us to listen and follow his guide. On this day, running with my dog, I heard Him and I yielded some-what, but not completely.

In my first near-death experience, I felt transported to another realm and experienced the freedom I felt of letting go completely. I felt the pain and struggle (my will) lifted out of me. My challenge is that I keep fighting to take it back. I know, of course, that I'm not the only one who struggles with some form of willfulness and control. How do we truly let go of those things in our life that keep us from being the best version of ourselves?

We all have indicators in life that tell us to listen and stop certain harmful behaviors. Sometimes we listen and sometimes we don't. Today, I feel closer to letting go than I did yesterday. I am open to completely letting go of my patterns of self disser-vice. I am not, however, free of them. We do best when we seek to move in the direction of progress versus perfection in any challenge we face. In this recent experience with Rigley, I slowed down and was aware that I was off. I was more in touch with my heart. That's progress.

I still have the urge to push through the discomfort as I did as a young skater and later in competing in races. In fact, I now help women learn to challenge their discomfort and work though physical, emotional, and spiritual pain. I use my gifts and personal struggle to help them grow into their best selves and get to the other side of discomfort.

None of us are ever done in becoming the best we can be. My struggle with exercise is still with me as I complete this story. My hope is that when I am talking to you another time, I will feel different. If not, I am hopeful that I will continue to be willing to see the path God has for me to follow and accept new patterns as a pathway to inner peace and joy.

I am aware that my heart may stop again during exercise. I make sure I am well hydrated, ease into all workouts, and take an inventory of how I am feeling along the way. While I used to push through or ignore what my body was telling me, I now pay close attention to and listen to my body. I respect my body's limitations although I do not like them right now. I do miss competing, but I am learning how to navigate new life goals of living and no longer running (all the time) from my life.

I have a greater appreciation for the people, places, and things that are in my life. I enjoy simple experiences and inter-actions with friends, family, and clients. My mom and I have been able to work through many of those past struggles and have come out the other side—our relationship has gotten so much better. My brother, Ryan, is living in a group home with men who have similar challenges. He has a job and loves competing in the Special Olympics (one of us made it!). We talk on the phone often, and I'm grateful I can be a part of his life. And most importantly, my relationships with Pat, Megan, and Kevin have matured. My heart has opened in a way that I never could have imagined.

My business is changing and growing in new areas. I am helping more women who suffer inside quietly, while trying to show up on the outside. I am more available to help others. As

I get out of myself, I can see that we are all hurting and I can be there to listen, share and help. I'm no longer running from the past...I'm excited for the future!

I feel a greater sense of peace and overall well-being most of the time. It can be challenging to hold onto to this, however. I can be tripped up by a life circumstance or events that arise unexpectedly, but I regroup more easily. My outlook has shifted into a bit more "go with the flow" rhythm versus a strict nonstop daily order of events that I had previously followed. That order gave me an illusion of control but I was missing out on some really good stuff.

I feel a bit softer and more flexible for the most part. I am attempting to live a more authentic and real life, with a goal of living life on life's terms one day at a time. I have a new sense of awareness that I am not in control of my life or anyone else's. God is winning my internal tug of war. In the days and weeks to come, I will struggle to win back control, but His hold is growing stronger than mine. I feel truly blessed to be alive for one more day. God's plan for me and each of us is beyond our imagination, if we can only let go and allow Him to do His work in and through us. I am enough.

WITH MEGAN (TOP) AND KEVIN

peace prayer of saint francis

Lord, make me an instrument of your peace:
where there is hatred, let me sow love;
where there is injury, pardon;
where there is doubt, faith;
where there is despair, hope;
where there is darkness, light;
where there is sadness, joy.

O divine Master, grant that I may not so much seek
to be consoled as to console,
to be understood as to understand,
to be loved as to love.
For it is in giving that we receive,
it is in pardoning that we are pardoned,
and it is in dying that we are born to eternal life.
Amen.

about kristin

Kristin DiDomenico is the owner of Kristinfitness, a personal training and health coaching business based in northern Virginia. She is an AFFA certified personal trainer and certified holistic health counselor. For the past 20 years, she has been training, educating and motivating people to live their best life through her personalized health and fitness programs.

Kristin became a health and nutrition counselor to help women improve their eating habits and break cycles of addictive and emotional eating in order to develop and maintain a healthy weight and a positive relationship with food. She received her health coach training at the Institute for Integrative Nutrition in New York City.

Kristin offers individual and group health, fitness and nutrition coaching for busy female professionals and moms, both in person and online. Learn more at kristinfitness.com. Kristin lives in Potomac Falls, Virginia with her husband, Pat and two children, Megan and Kevin and dog, Rigley.

22791246R00073

Made in the USA
Middletown, DE
15 December 2018